£2 00

George Mason.

D1493253

SOME MEMORIES

SOME MEMORIES

by

EUSTACE PERCY

1958

EYRE & SPOTTISWOODE

LONDON

Foreword

Except for the very few who have made their own life a work of art, autobiography is justified only as raw material for history. I hesitate to plead that justification because, though I have lived a good deal on the fringe, at least, of great events, I have kept no diary and preserved no correspondence; and, though I have a good memory, experience has taught me to distrust it for the purposes of serious history. For instance, in 1915, as a clerk in the Foreign Office, I wrote for the Cabinet a detailed survey of British diplomacy in the Balkans since the outbreak of war. Five or six years later, when I no longer had access to what I had written, I tried to reproduce its main outlines in an article which, fortunately, I did not publish. In 1925, as a Cabinet Minister, I read again my original memorandum, only to find that my draft article was just wrong enough to distort the sequence of events. Nothing can more subtly muddy the waters of history than first-hand evidence unchecked by documents.

Nor is this the worst snare that the memoir-writer sets for the future historian. A reminiscence may be accurate without being trustworthy. Especially in the modern age of publicity and mixed company, every statesman puts himself hourly on record, or gives himself away in after-dinner argument. For instance, a contemporary historian has quoted Sir Austen Chamberlain as saying, about the time of Locarno, that the British people would never go to war to preserve the western frontier of Poland. No doubt the reminiscence is verbally accurate; but I do not recognize in it the grounds upon which Sir Austen actually justified his Locarno policy to his colleagues. To go no further, he was too seasoned a politician, in the better sense of the word, not to remember Napoleon III's rebuke of a parliamentary indiscretion by his Minister: *en politique on ne dit pas jamais*. He may have been wrong

7

to leave open the issue of the indivisibility of European security; but he did deliberately intend to leave it wide open. This sort of misrepresentation is one to which minor actors on the fringe of the scene are particularly prone.

Yet there is, perhaps, one sort of history to which such an actor may contribute. The purpose of all history is human measurement. In detail, it is the measurement of individual men in action; and, for that, the only reliable sources are original documents. But, in gross, it is also the measurement of social shapes and movements; including the shapes and movements of governments. In that kind of history, original documents are less reliable, for, whether in private diaries or letters or the public press, they tend to be little more than 'still' snapshots of a constantly moving scene. There, then, the mere autobiographical essayist may have his uses, and he may even be a better witness to some scenes he has watched than to others in which he has acted.

But it would be dishonest to pretend that these memoirs are an aloofly impersonal contribution to history. If my life is, in itself, of no interest to the world, it is of interest to me, and I have no doubt that, on paper, I have made more of it than it deserves. More dangerously, I have no doubt that I have made it more coherent than it has been in fact. It has been largely a life of loose ends, of unfinished beginnings, and I fear I may not have resisted the temptation to patch it into a pattern which may flatter it. I may have done this patching in a way that has twisted my view of the history of my times, and against this the reader should be on his guard.

One temptation, however, I hope I have resisted: to bring my commentaries too much up-to-date. I have, for instance, commented a good deal upon Egypt and the Suez Canal; but most of these passages were written before the summer of 1956, and I have added little to point the moral of these latter days. I have, indeed, added something, where the moral has seemed too obvious to be ignored; but I have tried to make it easy for the reader to discount these additions, if he wishes, as the moralizings of an outsider, long divorced from actual contact with issues of policy.

CHAPTER I

Before 1914: The "Old Order"

I

At the outset, I may almost be said to have watched from outside even the world of my own youth. Born in 1887 with the biggest of all possible silver spoons in my mouth, and leaving Oxford in 1907 with something of the reputation of an infant prodigy, I seemed natural heir to the spaciousness of Edwardian and early Georgian England. Yet I spent much of the next two years, 1907–9, abroad, preparing for the diplomatic service, and the four years 1910–14 at my first post in Washington. Apart from boyhood impressions, therefore, it was a little through foreign field-glasses that I watched the last days of the Old Order, which has bulked so fabulously in the eyes of later generations.

It was not, of course, so fabulous as all that. Its scale of expenditure was, by modern standards, princely; but it seemed to breed in my contemporaries no particular taste for possessions or high living. The home of my childhood was, no doubt, not typical, though perhaps not more untypical, at one extreme, than, at the other, for instance, the Blenheim described so unsympathetically in Madame de Balsan's recent memoirs. It belonged, moreover, to the seventies of the century rather than to the nineties, for, as the twelfth of thirteen children, I inherited a long-established pattern of family life. But "aristocracy", anyway, does not run to types, and its best fruits are apt to be a little out of season. A mild bent towards eccentricity and anachronism is, indeed, its virtue and its only salvation.

Apart from intimacies not to be written, my chief impression of my parents is of an immensely laborious life, lived increasingly, as they grew older, "against the collar". Both my father and my mother must have habitually come near to Peel's daily routine as Prime Minister: six hours at the writing desk. Of my mother, indeed, this was probably true only of the last fifteen years or so of her life, when she had full charge of three great country houses, their households and their parish pumps, and when her youngest children were growing up. Before then, she had been more than fully occupied with the cares of the nursery and the schoolroom, for, in spite of a full complement of "nannies" and governesses, she had, for thirty years, assumed personal charge of her children to a degree which would astonish some of the present generation. She had nursed them through all their illnesses, had borne them company, and had played a significant part in their early education, at least in the old-fashioned manner of reading good literature to them and encouraging them to learn poetry by heart. It was not until she had been partly relieved of these cares that she had time to devote herself to such outside business as the founding and administration of a County Nursing Association, and the like. Still, even before that, constant correspondence with her large family must have tied her closely to her writing desk.

It was a disciplined home, of the kind that social historians like to classify as "evangelical"; but the classification is, perhaps, a little obtuse. Gospel Christianity relies on stronger incentives to a godly life than family codes of conduct. The motive of the parental strictness of those days, which underlay so essentially free and happy a family life, was usually a shrewder fear of the infectious idleness that haunts a leisured society. We were brought up, for instance, to hunt, but also to observe that the comic ugliness of Jorrocks and Sponge may be unpleasantly true to life, and that, outside Ireland, Flurry Knox ceases to be a joke. The choice of a definite profession was constantly urged upon us. This fear of the "waster" had, no doubt, its disadvantages. In discouraging dilettantism, it may have done something to repress culture and thus to rob leisure of its best savour. In the last decade of the Old Order, the grace of Lutyens' country villas, built for gardens and weekends, may have been a significant, even a healthy, reaction against the stuffiness of the great houses. But let it be remembered, at least, that, in those houses, Kipling's "lordliest life on earth" was far from being "effortless".

Nor was it "unthinking" or careless of the future. Whatever privileges my generation enjoyed in its youth, a sense of security was not one of them. It was at least as overshadowed by premonitions of catastrophe as the rather self-pitying generation, born twenty-five or thirty years later, whose traces I found still lingering in a northern university in 1937, though it was then already giving place to lustier successors. I remember no time, after I began at all to think for myself, when a European war did not seem to me the most probable of prospects, or when I forgot my first ugly taste of public disaster in the Black Week of Colenso and Magersfontein, which had darkened the Christmas school holidays of 1899. I think I always felt, too, that there had been something spectral about the brilliant group of royal uniforms that, as a privileged Eton boy, I had watched, a year later at Windsor, file slowly past me, almost within arm's length, behind Queen Victoria's coffin, in the damp dusk of a January afternoon.

It was, perhaps, not good for one's political education that, while war was thus the shadow on the future, the idea of positive political action, as it was presented to me in the Oxford of 1904–7, was so entirely concerned with domestic issues of "social reform". These were the years of the Russo-Japanese War, the first Moroccan crisis and the Anglo-Russian Entente of 1907; but they were also, and to a young man more tangibly, the years of unemployment, of a new interest in housing and poor law reform, and of the nascent ideas about what was later to be called a "planned economy" – as then diversely conceived by the young Beveridge, the I.L.P., the Chamberlainite Tariff Reformers, and the new school of Christian socialism. It was this last and most emotional interpretation that made, I think, the strongest impression on my callowness.

Yet, if one is inclined to question the political influence of this Oxford, one must remember that an influence of this kind must be judged by those who allow themselves to be really "dyed in the wool" by it, rather than by those who, like myself, are content merely to be coloured at the edges by a tincture of it. The Oxford of the "social gospel" did produce one Prime Minister who will occupy a special place in history. Clement Attlee was my senior by some years and I never met him in those days; but he has always seemed to me the typical son of the Oxford I knew.

2

All this does not mean that we took ourselves too seriously. It certainly never occurred to my generation to regard ourselves as members of a hereditary "governing class"; and that muddle-headed phrase has never ceased to irritate me. It is a commonplace that, in the last quarter of the nineteenth century, the era of agricultural depression and of Gladstone's Civil Service, the great landowning families ceased to govern England. But in what sense had they ever done so? They had been, at least until 1832, the leaders of a powerful electoral "interest"; but less powerful, on the whole, because less politically united, than a dozen Washington "lobbies" in the United States of Theodore Roosevelt; and both Pitts had shown that it could be as successfully challenged. Many such families had been founded by active politicians or public servants; but these founders had themselves been hardly more than squires, if that; and their richer descendants, though constantly on the fringes of national government, were seldom at its centre. Only by the rarest of chances did a great house like Hatfield revive its primitive glories. Indeed, when one considers the Whig Opposition in the wilderness at the turn of the eighteenth and nineteenth centuries, as it circled round Holland and Devonshire and Carlton Houses, one is almost tempted to the paradox that only by ceasing to govern could a group of politically minded families ever succeed, for a generation or so, in making itself look like a governing class.

A landed estate is an engrossing business, even when it is small enough to be a hobby. Early in the eighteenth century, the modest cares of Houghton might offer a convenient base for Walpole's career of government, but, towards its end, Shelburne was a little too much the Lord of Bowood to be effective at Westminster. In the nineteenth century, only an extraordinary combination of circumstances could detach even Lord Grey from his beloved woods at Howick, and then only for the brief crisis of the Reform Bill. Much more, Lord Derby's three short premierships had the air almost of amateur interludes in the more serious affairs of Lancashire. In fact, there is a general truth in Burke's tilt against the Duke of Bedford in 1796: in the contrast he drew between the imposing structure of national government on the hill of "the British Zion" and "the mounds and dykes of the low fat Bedford level". The real governors of England were always whole-time professionals; and, in Burke's day, at the height of the parliamentary oligarchy, it was increasingly in the immediate suburbs of Zion that they took their ease. Any group of professionals who are "at it the whole time" tends to become a social clique, whether it is composed of clubmen or trade unionists. The Lutyens villadom was not, after all, a bad reproduction, in modern terms, of the leisure that these professionals had enjoyed in such suburbs, at Putney or Clapham, Chiswick or Twickenham, or even as far afield as Brocket and Broadlands, untroubled by the provincial splendours and responsibilities of Knowsley, Welbeck or Belvoir, Chatsworth or Holkham.

In their provinces, these Dukes of Omnium might, I suppose be fairly described as a "governing class", but not more so than the gentry on whom fell most of the drudgery of county business. In that busy little world of the Quorum and Quarter Sessions, their central influence was oddly intangible. At its best, it was derived from a genuine reputation for disinterestedness; at its worst, it rested sometimes on a mere Double Alibi, as in the gibe levelled at a competent, if not brilliant, politician of my youth that he carried weight in London only because he was thought to have influence in ——shire, and in ——shire only because he was thought to have influence in London. In Northumberland, at any rate, the Smithsons who had brought the Percy name and tradition back to Alnwick in the first years of George III, after a hundred years' absence,[1] had come of no very different stock from the new squirearchy of Tyneside business men, who had been establishing themselves on the ruins of the old Jacobite families since the beginning of the century. When, a few years later, these new Percies had stretched their influence too far in a disputed county election, a local lampoonist had hastened to remind them, in an imitation of Horace, that

> "No fruit of Smithson's feeble loins
> Ere dyed the Tweed in Scottish blood."

Hardly less than the earlier Russells, who had made their Bedford level by drainage of the fens, the new Percies, like the new squires, had found their main field of activity in local economics, rather than in even local politics. They had had to restore a derelict agriculture and to develop the coalfields whose ownership the old Percies had successfully asserted against the Crown in the reign of Elizabeth I. Their importance declined as their economic function became attenuated, as they became the good managers, rather than the enterprising developers, of their estates and royalty owners instead of mining promoters.

Curiously enough, on the other hand, in county government they became, for a moment at least, more important at the end of the nineteenth century than they had been at its beginning. At its beginning, in November 1803, the old soldier who was then Duke of Northumberland had complained that even his Lord Lieutenancy had been practically put into commission in a caucus of deputy lieutenants, and he could only grumble impotently, in almost the same words as the critics of the Home Guard in 1940, over the absurdities of a scheme of coast defence by "Sea Fencibles, armed with pikes and disposed in bands of from eighteen to thirty and forty, over a tract of one hundred miles." But, at its end, the reorganization of county government between 1888 and 1902 imposed on his heirs a growing burden of direct administrative

---

[1] The hundred years, in strict fact, had ended in the previous generation, when the Hertfords had resumed residence, though without assuming much local responsibility.

responsibility; and, at the turn of the century, my father found in the new mixed local democracy of the agricultural and mining communities, over which he presided as Chairman of the County Council from 1895 until his death in 1918, the heaviest and, I think the most congenial work of his life. It was never more congenial than when, at its end, in another war, he found himself, in contrast to his ancestor, also responsible, if only honorifically, for the Territorial Army of his county.

I was amused recently to read in one of Beatrice Webb's published diaries that, after a glimpse of him at luncheon at Alnwick in 1906, she noted him as a man of little intelligence "entombed" in a sort of feudal isolation. This seems to me to be a characteristic misjudgment of life by a publicist immersed in "policies". I wonder what she might have thought if she had seen him at his work at the Moot Hall at Newcastle – or, for the matter of that, in the society of physical scientists at the Royal Institution in London, whose company he loved and among whom he was favourably known.

3

It was natural that such county administration should be congenial to such men as my father. The grain of truth in this talk of a governing class is the obvious one that large private responsibilities do tend to form in their possessors a certain talent for public affairs. A certain talent, but one that is apt to be restricted in its range. In the landowner, great or small, it tended to be essentially personal, best employed in affairs which he could know and measure by sight and touch. He could manage men with whom he could talk, but he was uncertain in judging public opinion or in conducting public debate. More fundamentally, his very vivid moral sense was one of personal duty to a personal neighbour, whether his equal or his dependent; what is now called a "social conscience" would have seemed to him dangerously irresponsible, because impersonal. He belonged, indeed, to a "service", rather than to a "governing", class – and even more genuinely so thirty years after the abolition of "purchase" in the army. It was a class that

bred good regimental and ships' officers in the army and navy, but
not so often good staff officers; good parish parsons, but not so
often good bishops of a State Church; good Indian civil servants
who were more at home in their districts than at Simla; and, for
the same reason, good local administrators who were more at
home in County Councils than in Parliament.

Mr. G. M. Young has somewhere remarked that the Civil Service inherits much of its special *moral* from an era when gentlemen-
Ministers handled their departments in Whitehall as they were
used to handle their estate offices at home. Such men had not
seldom large views on problems of government, but their views
were then usually out of scale both with their executive competence and with their moral standards. Hence the characteristic
barrenness of aristocratic radicalism; it so rarely achieved the
fusion of the ideal and the practical which makes a policy. Even
when that fusion was achieved, as in Lord Durham's Report on
the government of Canada, or in Gladstone's reform of the
machinery of parliamentary government at home, its achievement
was usually due to exceptional secretaries or civil servants – to
Charles Buller and Charles Trevelyan, rather than to Radical Jack
or the G.O.M. himself. And among the great Foreign Ministers,
the Castlereagh–Salisbury tradition of limited aims in foreign
policy, whether it was better or worse than the more imaginative
Canning–Palmerston tradition, was certainly the more true to
type. It was, at any rate, typical of Tories like my father, who took
pleasure, at the height of fashionable "imperialism", in professing
himself a "little Englander", even a "pro-Boer", and in quoting
the text: "the eyes of the fool are in the ends of the earth".

Perhaps the best example of this limited talent in the Old Order
was what may be regarded as its final display in the Balfour
Government of 1902–5, under which I began to grow up. In it,
the Cecil–Balfour–Lyttelton connection created, for the last time,
the illusion of government by a group of "ruling families".
Austen Chamberlain was fond of telling me, in his reminiscent
moods, that justice had never been done to the record of that
government, for it had after all provided, in three years, durable,

if modest, solutions of four major problems: Education, Licensing, Irish Land and Anglo-French relations. But its most significant feature was surely the contrast between the workmanlike competence of Wyndham's Irish Land Purchase Act and the amateurishness of his Irish "Devolution" scheme on which he made his shipwreck. And there was the same sort of contrast between Curzon's impressive administrative achievement, during his first five years as Viceroy of India, and the miscalculations of his quarrel with Kitchener, which caused his downfall.

Yet, after all, these limitations were characteristic, not so much of any Old Order, as simply of a limited administrative experience. Apart from all distinctions of class or wealth, or even of country, few municipal reputations survive in national politics – witness the late M. Herriot in France and a dozen reform mayors of American cities in the early years of the twentieth century. In the 1920s, civil servants who liked and admired Neville Chamberlain were wont to attribute his spectacular failure in the Ministry of National Service in 1917 to his mayoral habit of treating a department in Whitehall as the affair of himself and one town clerk. Perhaps he never quite unlearnt that habit. No doubt, this dependence on the personal touch has not quite the same flavour in a city mayor as in a county magnate; but in both instances it has the same sort of municipal excellencies and is the same sort of handicap in the wider fields of national and imperial policy. It has proved an even worse handicap in the international field, in the modern age of "global security" and the war of ideologies.

Indeed, such dependence is simply the characteristic of the educated Englishman, wherever he appears in the continual shifting and overlapping of classes which has made English social history. His genius for government and the bent of his education have always lain in his instinct to translate political principles into terms of personal relationships and personal responsibilities. That is certainly not less true of the trade-union-trained Labour politician of today than of his Tory predecessor. The most spectacular example of this limited talent in recent times was surely Mr. Ernest Bevin's monumental failure in the question of Palestine.

B

Sometimes, of course, this instinct fails, and sensitiveness to personal relationships gets lost in an ideology. But it is odd how temporary these lapses have been. One instance was the typical Puritan of the seventeeth century; another, I think, was the typical member of the Liberal Party, as it emerged from the new electorates of the second and third Reform Acts. That may have been why, in the last thirty years of the Old Order, party politics acquired a special tang of bitterness, more characteristic of the competing ideologies of continental "democracy" than of the English parliamentary tradition. Perhaps, at bottom, the resulting temperamental cleavage between two sorts of educated Englishman had more to do with the Liberal Unionist secession, and with the eclipse of Liberalism after 1918, than any issue of policy. Certainly, it had much to do with the decline in the dignity and prestige of the House of Commons in the last decade of the Old Order. Viewed at a distance, as I had to view it from Washington, that decline seemed the most ominous feature of the years before 1914.

Indeed, one is sometimes tempted to think that it was a governing Liberal ideology, rather than any governing class, that was the real distinguishing characteristic of the last days of the Old Order – the only element in it that, for good or ill, could not survive the first war as a distinct political force or a distinct school of statecraft.

4

But there was, be it confessed, another element in the bitterness of pre-1914 politics. The traditionally educated Englishman's instinct for personal relationships, with his consequent distrust of the "doctrinaire", has always had its seamy side. He has had, characteristically, a curious superficial trick of public arrogance outside the immediate range of his personal contacts, which may be combined with the most genuine modesty within that range. The classic example of this trick in English history is, perhaps, the flat contradiction between the damning public reputation of Castlereagh and the almost universal affection felt for him among all who worked with him personally. But, however superficial this trick may be, the historian is bound to take it seriously. In the gallery of English "Pride and Prejudice", he can be content to shrug his shoulders over Lady Catherine de Burgh; but Mr. Darcy is the caricature of something altogether more dangerous. It is all very well for Miss Elizabeth Bennet to protest that: "he has no improper pride"; but the fact remains that the impression made by his public manners on people outside his immediate circle was largely responsible for the bitterness of Tory-Radical politics before 1914, and did much, over more than a century, to bedevil both Anglo-Irish and Anglo-American relations.

Of Anglo-American relations I shall have much to say later. Of pre-1914 party politics or of Ireland I am hardly qualified to speak. But I have never forgotten the sick, almost epileptic, hatred in the face of a chance-met Liberal during my first parliamentary election in 1919, when he spoke of an old encounter with my father, in some matter of provincial politics, and made it clear that he intended to continue the feud with me. Nor can I forget the first Cabinet Committee I attended, in 1923. It met to receive an Eire Cabinet Minister who wished to explain the new land purchase legislation contemplated by his government. I attended only because I was then, for the moment, chairman of a Treasury Committee investigating the same problem in Northern Ireland. The Eire proposals were generous and argued considerable political courage, but the Minister was ill at ease and personally unimpressive; and I was ashamed at what I can only call the instinctive ungraciousness of his reception.

Later, on the front bench of the House of Commons, I came to realize how easily I myself could, in the same way, offend men of the Opposition, like George Lansbury, who, outside the Chamber, were not far from being my personal friends. That failing disabled me from ever becoming a "good House of Commons man". A Conservative elder, with whom I had to cross swords over the Government of India Bill in 1935, diagnosed it, a little unkindly, as the symptom of a "frustrated pontifical vocation". Perhaps that is as good a description as any of a certain tone in public business which appears, however unintentionally, to assume an authority, intellectual or moral, outside the always narrow personal circle within which ordinary men can expect such authority to be accepted.

I am afraid, too, that this capacity for giving offence was enhanced, in my generation, by a certain decay in mere manners. What had been known as "good society" was in a state of disintegration; the tone of a no longer really leisured class was being set by its younger, rather than by its eldest, sons; and, in consequence, the manners of the "nobility and gentry" (to use the phrase of a much earlier day) were becoming the manners of the club and of the mess, rather than of the drawing-room. Attentive readers of *Pride and Prejudice* will have observed that, even in 1813, a country gentlewoman like Miss Austen evidently preferred the manners of Mr. Gardiner, the City merchant, to those of either Mr. Bennet or Mr. Darcy. Three or four generations later, when the two strains had had time to mature or run to seed, there could be no doubt that Mr. Gardiner's descendants, wherever they had remained faithful to their urban origins, usually in provincial cities like Birmingham or Liverpool, and had resisted the temptation to become country gentlemen, had the advantage over Mr. Darcy's, not only in company manners, but also in a cultivated taste for the amenities of life, for food and wine and books and conversation. In fact, the right to the description "well-bred", for what it is worth, had passed to them. And they knew it. "In my old friend Huxley's time," says G. K. Chesterton's country doctor of 1913 or thereabouts, "we of the middle classes disbelieved in reason and all sorts of things. But we did believe in good manners. It is a pity if the aristocracy can't." That was the feeling, not only of Mr. Gardiner's descendants, but of many New England and Canadian friends of my youth; it was the feeling of Smuts when he said that the two problems of South Africa were the ignorance of the backveldt Boer and the arrogance of the English; and it was the regretful feeling, too, of my own parents, who impressed on me constantly, with however little success, the superiority of English "middle-class" manners. And, if Eton and the more fashionable colleges of Oxford in my day were good schools of character, I doubt if they were ever good schools of manners. That fact might be usefully considered today by educational reformers who wish to substitute large "comprehensive" establishments of secondary education for modest-sized grammar schools. It is not good for anyone's social manners or social habits to be educated in a crowd.

CHAPTER II

Before 1914: Washington, 1910-14

I

The American scene bulks very large in my memories. For one thing, it was the scene where I began my working life, and of such scenes it is written:

"We've only one virginity to lose
And where we lost it, there our hearts will be."

For another, it took, in some sort, the place of school and university as the birth-place of my lasting friendships; for, much as I have loved Oxford, it became too early to me, as to most of my generation, a place of ghosts.

And, by way of background to work and friendship, it was in America that I first tasted the excitement of natural beauty. I reached Washington on the brilliant afternoon of May 6, 1910, the day of King Edward's death, and, from that moment, fell a life-long victim, like an earlier visitor fresh from England more than forty years before, to "the charm of Washington spring. Education for education, none ever compared with the delight of this".[1] In one's calf country, even if it is as wildly lovely as my native Northumberland, Nature is a familiar presence, a friend whom one takes for granted. It is a new experience to be startled by her - not only in her moments of extravagance as in the crude finery of the Arizona desert, but, even more, in the ordinary changes of her seasons: dressed in the simple dogwoods and judas of a Virginian April, or flaunting the gypsy scarlets of a New Hampshire fall, or magicked into a forest magnolia at dusk in an Alabama woodland, in full blossom and pulsing with fireflies.

[1] *The Education of Henry Adams.*

But, indeed, Nature apart, excitement is, to a young man, the prevailing climate of American life. Not that, to a careful observer, it breeds more novelty than other countries, but every novelty has a freer field. In those days, at least – the days for instance, of Henry Ford's pioneering experiments in mass production and of the "Progressive" revolt in the Republican Party – the new did not, as in England, work quietly to modify the accumulated achievements of the past; it placarded itself and all presumptions were in its favour. Except in the two favourite fields of serious American thought, technology and jurisprudence, discovery hardly had to prove its originality or staying power before it began to displace established ideas and practices. One consequence of this rather uncritical exuberance was that it was difficult to distinguish real from false originality. Looking back, I can now see, for instance, that I overrated the significance of political reform movements and labour unrest, and underrated that of technological research and organization. Another consequence was that the only administrative virtue recognized by Americans tended to be "drive", and that tendency did more than any political "spoils" system to discourage the growth of a regular American civil service and to discredit the English civil service in American eyes. Because I found all this exhilarating and congenial, I have been, ever since, a fairly good judge of American politics and have always found it easy to work with Americans; but it was a doubtful training for European diplomacy and a dangerous one for English politics.

In this rather undergraduate mood of mine, my first and much-loved chief, James Bryce, was a delight. To me, he was very like an Oxford tutor. His interests were encyclopaedic, the tale of his travels Odyssean, and his views in some ways surprising. Turkey and the Balkans seemed to be the only subject on which his opinions conformed to any recognized Liberal pattern. Conservatives at Westminster who, in 1911, the year of the Canadian Reciprocity controversy, rated him as a weak admirer of the United States and as something of a traitor to the British Empire, were widely far from the mark. He was, in fact, a much more

ardent imperialist than my Tory father, and much more critical of
the United States than, I think, Joseph Chamberlain had been. He
had always, he told me in my first summer, refused to attend
Fourth of July celebrations, "regarding the Declaration of Independence, as I do, as an unmitigated disaster to both countries."
He was shocked by the pro-American bias of Sir George Otto
Trevelyan's *History of the American Revolution*. He thought the
Pacific slope no natural part of the United States and regretted
that British Columbia had not been extended into Oregon and
California on the break-up of the Spanish Empire. He could not
forgive the shade of General Whitelocke for having failed to make
the Argentine a British territory. In social philosophy, he abominated Herbert Spencer, and the only young men he ever lost
patience with were earnest Latin American Ph.D. students who
sent him for approval their adulatory theses on that, to him,
"monumental humbug".

He had also the agelessness and the endearing eccentricities
traditionally associated with university dons. At seventy-five he
could outwalk me on any mountain, frisking, into the bargain,
hither and thither after botanical specimens that caught his eye;
and he would swim lustily in a Maine lake on an afternoon in late
September, when we young men found it cold enough ashore. At
work, I remember him best struggling to clear a space among the
litter of galley-proofs on his desk for the revision of a draft
dispatch, or scrambling up his library shelves to find some item of
personal correspondence, which it was his squirrel-like habit to
secrete behind particular books, according to some private filing
system all his own.

One other ageless figure stands near the centre of my American
memories: Judge Holmes of the Supreme Court. My closest
friends during the latter half of my time in Washington were
among the young lawyers who used to sit at his feet, and I became
an anomalous member of that circle. Its most senior honorary
member asked me the other day how I rated Holmes in retrospect
because, since his death, it had become somewhat the fashion in
America to write him off as a "materialist". He has become cele-

brated enough outside the United States to make the question worth a considered answer. His mind was a kind of grand alliance (for it moved always in the grand manner) between the eighteenth-century sceptic and the nineteeth-century romantic. I confess that it was the romantic in him that most appealed to me – not the jurist and wit whom the world has come to know from his Court judgments and from so much of his published correspondence, but the veteran of the Civil War who emerged only in private talk and in his less known Memorial Day speeches and academic addresses. That, again, may have been too undergraduate a taste; but I think he would have approved it. The "liberalism" of his Court opinions was really a romantic refusal to subordinate life to the rigidities of legal art; his "materialism" was avowedly that of the romantic stoic who wrote the Book of Ecclesiastes. His most famous dissenting judgment, in defence of freedom of speech, has the tones of Carlyle rather than of Mansfield – "even if enough can be squeezed from these poor and puny anonymities to turn the colour of legal litmus paper". For all his scholarship, his heart was in a life of action. In one of my more Sidney-Webb moments, he threw off for my correction a phrase which he afterwards used in public: "education in the Obvious is of more importance than investigation into the Obscure"; and the most obvious to him was the maxim he once offered to Harvard undergraduates "in all sadness of conviction: that to think great thoughts you must be heroes as well as idealists".

2

My first three years in Washington covered the second half of the Bryce mission. That mission, celebrated in its day, has now receded into the middle distance of half a century or so, which tends to be the blind spot of history. It has been recorded by contemporaries as the turning point in modern Anglo-American relations, a point marked by the clearing up of a multitude of long-standing differences, from a disputed frontier on the barren coast of Maine to fishery rights in Newfoundland waters and the protection of fur seals in the North Pacific. The historians of the next generation will have to re-assess that record, and I think they will modify it materially.

The crucial corner in Anglo-American relations had, in fact, already been turned with the turn of the century, when John Hay had established with Lord Pauncefote a new tradition of intimate relations between the State Department and the British Embassy and had continued it, after Pauncefote's death, with that tragic inheritor of unfulfilled diplomatic renown, Sir Michael Herbert. Though the tradition had been interrupted during Sir Mortimer Durand's tenure at the Embassy in 1903–5, it was not difficult for Root and Bryce to take it up again where Hay and Herbert had left it. But this new Anglo-American intimacy had been little concerned with any settlement of old differences on the North American continent or its adjoining waters. The cleaning of that slate was necessary housemaid's work, but it was necessary to an improvement rather of Anglo-Canadian than of Anglo-American relations, for the inconclusive handling of these disputes by British diplomacy had been, for more than half a century, a standing grievance with Canadian opinion. What had concerned Hay was a much wider issue: what was to be America's choice of policies and friends in Europe and Eastern Asia in her first years of emergence as a world power, after the Spanish-American war? Diplomatically, Bryce's mission was something of a parochial interlude in these oecumenical pre-occupations. In my day, at least, we were little concerned in Washington with high international policy. Far Eastern affairs seemed quiescent, after the failure of Secretary Knox's Manchurian proposals in 1908; the Embassy held no more than a watching brief in the background of the Bankers' Consortium negotiations in 1911. Neither the Taft nor the Wilson administration showed any desire to follow the precedent of intervention in European crises which had been set by Theodore Roosevelt's rather irrelevant participation in the Algeciras Conference of 1906. We at the Embassy were conscious, in this connection, only of the steady wooing of American public men by the German Emperor, and we felt few qualms about our ability to compete with that.

Bryce's real contribution to the Hay-Pauncefote tradition was, so to speak, to convert the bank balance of Anglo-American intimacy, which had accumulated in the private diplomatic books at Washington, into an investment in American popular opinion. It could only be a long-range investment, for an ambassador could not give the impression of appealing directly to public opinion on current issues over the head of Congress; he must speak, as it was natural for Bryce to speak, academically and mainly to academic audiences; one might almost say that, in giving public evidence for his country, he could speak only as a witness to character. But, if the investment was a long-range one, it was real; while the diplomatic bank balance at Washington, however imposing it might look on paper, was essentially a blocked account, blocked by a Congress nearly always on the verge of insurrection against the administration of the day. The Bryce mission ended diplomatically in the fiasco of the draft Arbitration Treaty of 1911 and the lawyers' squabble of 1912 about Panama Canal tolls. The investment in public opinion, on the other hand, was to bring an astonishing, and an astonishingly early, return – how astonishing it is difficult to realize today.

My own astonishment is, perhaps trivially, identified in my memory with a contrasted anecdote and experience. For the anecdote, an old clerk at the Embassy, who had come there originally as Lord Pauncefote's butler, told me that the Union Jack had never been flown on the Embassy, for fear of hostile demonstrations, until one Fourth of July – I think in 1900 – when the ambassador found himself at a small hotel in New York State whose manager, an Englishman by origin, insisted on hoisting the flag, and did so with impunity. For the experience, I was to drive into Washington in April 1917 in the wake of President Wilson and Mr. Balfour, through cheering streets draped with Union Jacks, many of them mis-designed and nearly all of them upside down, but every one of them a touching symbol of respect and affection. Bryce's contribution to that revolution was, no doubt, infinitesimally small, but it had been, in its day, an original contribution.

Still, this friendly America had got its British flags all wrong – and that, too, was symbolic. What did not astonish me at all was that this revolution in popular feeling was so quickly followed, after the war, by a disastrous reaction. This is to run ahead of my story, but the public unpopularity of Britain in America in the nineteen-twenties seemed to me a wholly natural eruption of the old ill-feeling that I had found not far beneath the surface in the years immediately before 1914.

The existence and degree of that ill-feeling is now forgotten; but, in those years, it was as definite as the German popular resentments against England which played so large a part in bringing on the war – and hardly less threatening. One would have been wrong, indeed, to take too tragically the recurrent appearance in Anglo-American relations of the "big stick" and "shirt-sleeve diplomacy": for instance, the ugly smack of crude imperialism in some American speeches about Canadian Reciprocity, or the warning given me by my closest friend in Congress at that time, that "a fratricidal war" with Canada, at some date in the future, was a possibility to be seriously reckoned with. But it was all too evident that the United States had yet to choose her course as a world power; and Bryce expressed his deepest feelings when he once said to me that it was fortunate for the world that Americans did not yet know their strength, for when they did . . .

In those days, they were peculiarly uncertain of their strength in their new capacity as owners of overseas territories. On the one hand, in their tradition, "empire" was a sin and the chief sinners had been Spain and Britain. The Cuban and South African wars had intensified that tradition, the one setting the final seal on the Monroe Doctrine, the other suggesting, even to so cultivated a friend of John Hay as Henry Adams, a doubt whether the self-governing Dominions themselves were any longer safe, without American support, against the imperialism of Whitehall. In that mood, a colonial policy was abhorrent to them and they were anxious only to withdraw from Cuba and the Philippines at the earliest possible moment. On the other hand, by a more recent tradition, Americans had constituted themselves the patrons of a

China struggling towards "democracy"; they were inclined to champion that China against the "imperialism" of the Anglo-Japanese alliance, and to regard the Philippines as a kind of advanced base for an active Far Eastern policy. More realistically, the completion of the Panama Canal suggested, for its defence, a new strategic policy in the Caribbean, to be carried out by the then momentarily fashionable "dollar diplomacy", as in San Domingo, and by the retention or acquisition of naval bases, as in Cuba and the Virgin Islands. From these seeds of policy were to grow, in the fullness of time, the mixed fruits of a half-reluctant Anglo-American partnership in two wars: the liquidation in 1921 of the Anglo-Japanese alliance and, with it, of any secure basis for a Far Eastern policy by either partner; the independence of the Philippines; the building of an American fleet of long-range cruisers to compensate for lack of bases in the Pacific, which was the concealed cause of the collapse of the Geneva Conference of 1927; the leasing of American naval bases in the British West Indies; and, finally, Franklin Roosevelt's phantom pursuit, in his last days, of an understanding with Russia, based on a common opposition to British "colonialism". Whatever apprehensions one might have felt in 1910–14 about the long-range results of the old strain of American ill-feeling towards Britain, they would have fallen far short of this last portent: that a President of the United States, who almost passionately regarded the British Commonwealth of Nations as the chief guarantee of world peace and decency, should dream of a post-war policy directed to the liquidation of the British Empire in Asia and Africa.

3

This persistent ill-feeling deserves some further analysis, even if (as is even now not certain) it were only a curiosity of the past. Its re-appearance, in however modified a form, in the Suez crisis of 1956, has been an ominous warning of possible misunderstandings to come.

Would-be realists in England in the days of which I am writing, like Leo Maxse, used to identify this ill-feeling with the exotic

European elements in the American melting-pot, and consequently took pleasure in deriding the Anglo-Saxon platitudes of Pilgrim banquets. They were wrong. The name of England stood higher in the traditions of Slav and Italian immigrants than in those of one-hundred-per-cent Americans in New England or the Deep South – higher also among the sons and grandsons of the German exiles of 1848, though, during the war, their ancestral liberalism was to fight a losing battle with their ancestral loyalties – and highest of all among Jewish immigrants of all nationalities. Even among the Irish, the most intractable critics of Britain were often the least Celtic, the Protestant Ulstermen of the old pioneering stock, who had reached Illinois via Pennsylvania and Kentucky. No, the ill-feeling was, at root, a specifically Anglo-Saxon phenomenon. It was a special version of the old superstition about the English "governing class" over which I have already lamented in my first chapter.

This version was not unlike the favourite Belloc-Chesterton theme of the "gang" in English history since the Reformation, "the new grave lords who had eaten the abbeys' fruits". The Britain of George V, so Americans supposed, was still governed, as had been the Britain of George III, by a hereditary close corporation, which now comprised the landowners, the Universities of Oxford and Cambridge, the Established Church and the Civil Service. At the centre of this corporation was the "monarchy", which somehow symbolized its essentially reactionary character. Said the secretary of the Cigar Makers Union to me in his Chicago office at the beginning of a strike in 1910, when the men's leaders in Florida had been incontinently arrested and jailed, according to the then usual American routine in labour disputes: "We're up against a situation here that couldn't be duplicated even in monarchical England."

These governors of Britain were, according to this view, superficially clean; incorruptible in the ordinary sense, but impregnated with selfish economic interests; quite sincere in their high personal moral standards, but unscrupulous and diabolically clever in their diplomacy and their imperial policy. "I was very sorry to see, when I was in England," said W. J. Bryan when I first met him in the spring of 1911, "how completely both the Conservative Party and the Church of England had fallen under the corrupt domination of the brewers." "The aristocracy of England," shouted an ebullient Senator from Indiana at a Washington dinner table, expounding the Lloyd George Budget, "had never paid a penny in taxation since the Norman Conquest." All that, no doubt, was politicians' talk; and politicians' talk, too, was the bitter anti-British diatribe, in the older manner of New England, published by Senator Lodge in 1913, to celebrate the Hundred Years of Peace with England. What did seem to me serious was that, in my first summer, I found the same beliefs among the quiet tradespeople and professional men of a small Michigan town, whose Presbyterian minister was an old Rhodes Scholar friend of my Oxford days.

And, on occasion, I could not deny that there were elements of shrewdness in this curious jumble of ignorance and prejudice. Running, again, a little ahead of my story, the editor of the *Kansas City Star*, calling on me at the Foreign Office in the first winter of the 1914 war, thus described the views of his Mississippi Valley readers: "They don't know why the war began and they want it to end as soon as possible; but, on the other hand, they have an idea that the English governing class may make an easy and ignominious peace ... and they don't want that." Perhaps that did not then represent any real body of opinion; but the lurking suspicion that these hereditary rulers, for all their airs of superiority, might, at a pinch, prove "soft" was to crystallize twenty years later, into the very definite body of American opinion which reacted so violently against "appeasement" in Europe.

Their airs of superiority – I use those words deliberately, because they serve to introduce again the figure of Mr. Darcy, the eternally recurrent educated Englishman. As I have tried to describe him in my first chapter, he has been the oldest promoter of ill-feeling in America. I have diagnosed his offensiveness as a tendency to pontificate; but that is not the whole story.

The really unpardonable offence in public life is to pontificate in the territory of a rival pontiff. I should not, in my front-bench days, have given such offence to the Labour party if I had not had to defend policies which touched the lives of wage-earners so closely as education, school meals and juvenile unemployment; for the Labour party, by its very existence, claims an exclusive right to pontificate wherever working class interests are concerned. In the same way, the United States has always been the land of pontiffs, and Englishmen and Americans have always tended to pontificate in what each considered to be their own peculiar domain; the domain of moral principles in government. In the eighteen-twenties, Canning, whose kindest nickname in London was "the Pope", could not hope to compete amicably with a Boston high priest like John Quincy Adams in moral attitudes towards the new Spanish-American republics. Forty years later, Adams' son, as ambassador in London during the Civil War, was more exasperated by the moralities of an aristocratic liberal like Lord John Russell than was his colleague in Paris by the immoralities of all the gamblers of the Second Empire. Between those two famous episodes came the less remembered clash over Texas between the rival moralities of Aberdeen, the anti-slavery nobleman who had never seen a slave, and Calhoun, the child of tough Scotch-Irish yeomen who had pioneered on the frontier of a British slave colony.

The tragedy of the story is, indeed, that it is often the very best in Mr. Darcy that offends the best of Americans. That fact had emerged spectacularly, on the eve of Bryce's mission, in the unhappy episode of Sir Mortimer Durand, the ambassador who fell out with Theodore Roosevelt and was recalled by his government. Durand dreamed as fervently as Rhodes or Milner of a world governed by a partnership between the British Empire and the United States; but none of the three realized that imperial responsibilities were just the aspect of such a partnership for which Americans were still least prepared. Durand himself, formerly a famous Foreign Secretary of India and a dominating ambassador at Teheran, was the stateliest example of all that was most admirable in the old Indian proconsular tradition, but, as such, he typified the worst of Anglo-American moral conflicts. Americans thought proconsulship in itself immoral; Durand, for his part, was almost pathologically "of purer eyes than to behold iniquity": his rectitude winced, not only at the ordinary log-rollings of Congressional politics, but, even more, at the "sinister" side (the adjective was Bryce's) of Theodore Roosevelt himself. Wincing, he exaggerated the evil and he had been trained in the East not to conceal his repugnance, but to show it by a kind of haughty reticence.

That episode is a reminder that, in the long rivalry between British and American prides and prejudices, Mr. Darcy's silences have been more offensive than even his "Oxford accent". The special sting of his "arrogance" has always been his aloofness. In 1862, it was Russell's air of bland indifference to the building of blockade runners that provoked a New England ambassador to threaten war. In 1895, it was Salisbury's apparently Olympian neglect of American admonitions about Venezuela that stung President Cleveland, the honest son of a New York manse, into a fit of unnecessary bullying. In 1932, it was Sir John Simon's failure to explain his quite justifiable dislike of American proposals about Manchuria that so deeply wounded his fellow-lawyer, Mr. Stimson, the friendliest Secretary of State with whom an English Minister has ever had to deal. And, to come back to my own pre-war experience, there was something of the same irritating air of aloofness in the way that the Asquith Government in 1912, after long silence, discharged at President Taft the undiluted opinion of the Law Officers of the Crown on Panama Canal tolls, a document as smugly worded as are most lawyers' opinions.

Oddly enough, in Washington from 1913 onwards, Mr. Darcy could best see his own reflection in the mirror of Woodrow Wilson himself, as he can sometimes see it today in that impeccable graduate of Cambridge, Mr. Nehru. Wilson's ultimate failure with his own countrymen was partly due to the queerly English tone of his pontifications. To appear to be "too proud to fight" is precisely the quality in Mr. Darcy that an American Congressman

c

can least understand. Yet the best Englishmen have almost in-
variably made that mistake in their dealings with Americans.
"Don't argue with a man who isn't a gentleman when he loses his
temper," said Mr. Baldwin to me in 1928, when President
Coolidge had issued an ill-mannered statement about the Anglo-
French naval agreement and I had proposed, not a retort, but an
explanation of the facts. That seemed to me then, and still seems
to me now, to be the exact epitome of the characteristic attitude
which has most damaged Anglo-American relations throughout
their history.

4

In short, on the eve of the outbreak of war in 1914, the United
States was a dangerously uncertain factor as a world power; and a
close Anglo-American understanding seemed, in some ways, the
least probable outcome of its uncertainties. But it is significant
that, in making this point, I should have strayed so far from my
own experiences in pre-1914 Washington. I cannot pretend that,
in those days, I was much troubled by these doubts. I was too
happy in my excitements and my friendships, too much at home
in the kindliest country on earth. If I had been cross-examined
about the future, I think I should have expressed my feelings in
much the same language as Henry James, when he scribbled on
his application form for British citizenship in 1914 those words
about a "decent and dauntless people". I could not believe that the
fundamental common decency of the two peoples would allow
them, in the long run, to be other than friends.

Above all, I luxuriated in my almost unlimited freedom to
"come and go and look and know". That was unexpected, for the
Foreign Office tradition was that members of the Embassy at
Washington must be meticulously careful to avoid any appearance
of active interest in American internal affairs. But no one seemed
to mind when I entertained in my house a negro professor of
Howard University, or deserted the kindly, if oratorical, hospi-
tality of the city fathers of Mobile to stay for a weekend with
Booker Washington at his Tuskegee College. Or when I visited

the new Socialist city council of Milwaukee and made friends with Victor Berger, the lone socialist Congressman from that outpost of a very naïve Marxism. The nearest approach to a reproof was administered to me by old Henry Adams, who had frequented my grandfather's dinner table at Argyll Lodge in the London of the Civil War, when he told me that he supposed I couldn't help it, for my liking for "odd fish" was hereditary. I must have been the only diplomat who ever found himself helping to line Pennsylvania Avenue with Boy Scouts for a Presidential Inauguration. It was more remarkable, perhaps, that no one cared to notice in 1912 that I was living almost exclusively with supporters of Theodore Roosevelt and attended the Chicago Republican convention in their company. Certainly that vagary did not disturb my friendship with the Taft family or bar the White House to me.

What I did come to realize in all this freedom was that, in Washington at least, my friends and acquaintances tended to be confined to the governing class. For there is such a class in America – perhaps the only kind of governing class that really exists in any country: the men with executive experience of some kind, whether in big business, the law, the press or the Universities. The constitutional separation between executive and legislature has, in the United States, reproduced itself in something approaching a social distinction, as may be seen by anyone who compares the life histories of Presidents and their Cabinets with those of all but a very few members of the House of Representatives. Though Senators occupy a middle position – for, more often than not, they have had executive experience in their States and may be on their way to Cabinet office or even to the White House itself – I found the whole Capitol curiously impenetrable and its denizens, save for a few exceptional friends, uncomfortably on their guard. One met them, indeed, at Bryce's embassy and at other more or less formal dinner tables; one could meet them occasionally (if one was a mere junior) at luncheon or in the lobbies and offices on Capitol Hill, without exciting suspicions of intrigue; but only by meeting them on their native heaths, which might be two or three thousand miles from Washington, could one be sure of getting to know their real personalities or their real views.

Two men, who were to become leaders of the anti-British isolationists in the Senate between the wars, come especially to my mind in this connection. In 1911, I made bold to interview Hiram Johnson at San Francisco in the middle of his successful campaign as a reform candidate for governor and, though I think he was amused at me, nothing could have exceeded his kindness or his frankness; but when in 1917 I re-encountered him as a Senator in Washington, I found it impossible to renew acquaintance satisfactorily with him. Not till much later, in 1930, when I no longer had any shadow of an official position, did I get in touch momentarily with him again and found him as forthcoming and as sensible as he had been twenty years before. He was a sad example of a general truth, which makes half the tragedy of the Senate: that tough-minded men, whose executive talent is unemployed, easily turn stiff or sour in a parliament. The other half of the Senate tragedy was exemplified by Senator William Borah of Idaho. That same summer of 1911 I sought him out in his home town of Boise, to discuss his opposition to the Arbitration Treaty. I had known him at Washington in the houses of my "insurgent" Republican friends; but only then did he show me his real quality. He was an honest man, with a clear lawyer's head and some breadth of view, but a mutual friend once said of him that "the trouble about Bill is that he never does go over Niagara in that barrel". Membership of the Senate gives to soft-minded men like him, too sensitive for executive responsibility, a power of control over executive policy which they neither want, nor know how to use.

But, again, I am in danger of falsifying the picture of my pre-war years by painting in these political portraits. Even my working memories of those years are hardly political – least of all the memories of my special assignments outside the ordinary routine of the embassy. For instance: my first duty on arrival was the daily reading of the *Congressional Record*, from which I learnt little but that the speeches printed to be read by a Congressman's constitu-

ents had still something of the flavour of Elijah Pogram.[1] A year
later, I was told off to write a report for the Home Secretary,
Mr. Winston Churchill, on Mormonism. That gave me the
opportunity to see, in Salt Lake City, the most grandly sited city
in North America, and (in its older part) the best planned – and
to make the acquaintance of an impressive example of the
traditional "Southern Colonel", the editor of the local "Gentile"
paper, who had spent his life in fighting Mormonism, not for its
then already discarded practice of polygamy, but as the classic
type of what would now be called a "totalitarian" theocracy. Two
years later, I remember lobbying the chairman of the Senate
Tariff Committee on his verandah after breakfast one broiling
July morning about West Indian bananas. By that time, however,
Bryce had been succeeded by Sir Cecil Spring-Rice and real
diplomacy was beginning to break in on me, as the oldest sur-
viving though still the most junior, member of the regular
Embassy staff. That same July I was sent to Washington from our
summer embassy in New England, to discuss American policy in
Mexico with W. J. Bryan, as inconclusively as was usual with that
lovable but elusive troubadour of politics. But I soon relapsed,
the following winter, into such affairs as representing the Board of
Agriculture before an expert Committee of Inquiry on the
entrancing subject of black wart and pink scab in potatoes. Of
such, indeed, is the normal training of an attaché or Third
Secretary in the conduct of foreign relations.

5

Much more, my best memories are of life quite outside the
Embassy. I find it impossible to write of my friendships; instead,
let me try to sketch a few backgrounds.

I wish I had Sir Harold Nicolson's art of animated vignettes.
"Je voudrais, si ma vie etait encore à faire, habiter près d'un lac",

---

[1] I cannot resist recording the peroration of a speech which rewarded my first
day's reading: "The Rocky Mountains are as old as Mount Ararat, upon which
the Ark was permitted to rest, and as old as Mount Sinai, from whose lofty
summit was sung by stainless lips that grand refrain: 'peace on earth and goodwill
towards men'."

said Jeanne de Henaut, in the uncomfortably vivid conversation piece about his and my Parisian studies, which he included in his *Some People*. Well, I have had that experience and often feel homesick for a lake under a New Hampshire mountain – Dublin, where we twice had our summer embassy. It was a colony of summer residents, but not of the fashionable kind to which other embassies were wont to resort, on the "North Shore" of Massachusetts or at Bar Harbour in Maine. Many of the Dublin colonists had lived there for a generation and were accepted locally, if not as genuine natives, at least (in the complimentary idiom of New England) as "common" folk. I learnt to know there another characteristic element in the life of eastern America: the long summer holidays in half-wild country which had kept alive, for the youth of the wiser families of the governing class, something of the tradition of the "frontier", and had saved them from the English public schoolboy's tendency to depend for his amusement exclusively upon organized sport or games.

Those long lake-and-forest summers, especially one spent in 1912 in the more primitive recesses of Maine, gave me a habit which hardly suited my subsequent career: the habit of going to bed as soon as possible after dinner in order to begin my day as soon as possible after dawn. I found the charm irresistible of level sunlight through the birches, of a canoe creeping over mist-veiled water, and of "morning spread upon the mountains". I have never regretted that habit since my return to more domesticated surroundings, in spite of the consequent agonies of parliamentary life, for the English climate is at its best between five and eight o'clock in the morning. But when Bryce, who regarded breakfast about nine o'clock as the most social meal of the day came back from leave to stay with us at the end of that Maine summer, he found it hard to accommodate himself to a household returning famished at eight.

A very different background to friendship was Charlottesville, where I used to snatch weekends from Washington, to stay with another Rhodes scholar friend, who was then chaplain to the University of Virginia. In those days the University had not grown much beyond the long quadrangle of the original Jefferson design, with its lawn descending in shallow terraces between stumpy colonnades from the Library rotunda at its upper end to the open prospect of Monticello hill across the valley. The enchantment of old Virginia lingered over that lawn, and also the shadow of its tragedy – not, indeed the old colonial dominion of the eastern seaboard, but the premier state of the eighty years between Revolution and Civil War 1, for Monticello had been Jefferson's plantation home and the portrait of J. E. B. Stuart, Lee's cavalry leader, hung in the Library. For the curious stranger, both the enchantment and the shadow still took bodily form, not far from the university buildings, in the person of Miss Virginia Mason, last survivor of one of the greatest Virginian houses and a republican aristocrat after the high Roman fashion, albeit with a touch of Cranford about her. She used to hold simple court for a few university students in her cottage home, but . . . one must not mention Abraham Lincoln in her presence. And, nearby, there was a very different social survival in the poor whites of the Ragged Mountains, a huddle of wooded hills, lovely but stony-soiled, which had caught the backwash of the feeble or faint-hearted among the old pioneers in their slow advance over the Blue Ridge into the Shenandoah Valley. Inbred and riddled with tuberculosis, they were a pathetic remnant, among whom my friend had his little mission chapels, visited in long buggy drives on Sunday afternoons.

And then, of course, there is the background of Washington itself, the still half rural Washington whose back door opened directly on the Rock Creek woods and, at the distance of a short hour's tram journey, on the solitudes of the Potomac between Great Falls and the Seneca Rapids. In these surroundings, horse and canoe were the natural instruments of a young man's leisure, especially in the heats of late spring and early summer; but, of the two, I confess that I found the American version of the early ride a little over-strenuous. It was a serious exercise, taken at a pelting trot, or a hand gallop wherever the ground allowed, and I have, for instance, poignant memories of toiling in the wake of General

Leonard Wood and two aides over the sandy Virginian hills beyond Arlington on at least one July morning before breakfast.

Of Washington the city, my memories centre in the bachelor establishment, kept by a group of American friends, where I was often a visitor and where I lived during my last year. That household had a touch of du Maurier's Quartier Latin, with law and the erratic politics of the then infant *New Republic* taking the place of art as the focus of its endless talk and even more endless flow of casual guests. The range of our talk and our entertainment was "extensive and peculiar"; but we hardly took ourselves or our symposia seriously enough to deserve the mocking nickname of the "House of Truth" which some humourist conferred upon us.

One other vignette lives in my memory as a sort of old-fashioned woodcut at the end of a chapter: the central street of a Connecticut village, dreaming in the October sunlight of a Sunday afternoon in 1912. The papers had arrived at midday dinner with the news of the outbreak of the Balkan War. I escaped from my host's house to walk alone under the great elms which are the mark of the pioneer settlements of New England, as lime avenues are of some almost contemporary Whig mansions in old England. The news meant to me the first shots of a European war, but to the dwellers in this sleepy hollow, I thought, it meant, and could mean, nothing. Here, rather than in ancient England, was the real home of an immemorial and indestructible peace. I was both right and wrong – wrong because, hardly more than two years later, my host was to die tragically in London on his way to join an American Red Cross unit in France. It was to be the end of an American, no less than of a European, chapter; and in America, no less than in England, it was an Old Order that was passing.

CHAPTER III

War: Foreign Office and Washington

I

Daddy, what did you do in the Great War?
(Recruiting Poster 1914)

My son, I had a little chair,
Close by a little table set:
I sat there when the day was fair,
I sat there when the day was wet.

Fired with the glow of Pitt and Pam,
I wrote three little drafts a day,
And now and then a telegram
To cheer the heart of Edward Grey.

I wrote in secret registers
A lot of quite notorious things,
And noted how each fibre stirs
At platitudes from Balkan kings.

I . . . but, my son, you'll learn, no doubt,
A patriot's sacrifice is not
A thing one likes to brag about;
In fact, I . . . did a lot.

These verses, with others best expurgated, are, I suppose, still buried in the indestructible files of the Foreign Office, for the head of my department had them "jacketed" and sent them up the official ladder as far as a sense of humour would carry them. They are a fair description, if not of my work during the first year of the war, at least of my feelings about it. I had exchanged temporarily into the Foreign Office at the beginning of

June 1914, and August 4 found me in the Western Department, which was then merged with the Near Eastern Department to form the "War" Department.

I was set one personal task that August: to write the preface to the "Penny Blue Book", the popular version of the Command Paper containing the official correspondence of the Serbian crisis. In view of my subsequent very dim record as an author, it amuses me sometimes to think that, on the strength of that anonymous essay, I can probably claim to have been translated into more languages than any other Englishman of my time, even Bernard Shaw, that essay's most scornful critic.

But my chief memory of the War Department is that I learnt in it, after my enthusiastic American training, a new respect for red tape. The official files must contain another jacket, recording a blunder which still pricks my conscience. In war, a Foreign Office inevitably becomes something of a post office, transmitting urgently, and without question, the messages of Service Departments and their Cabinet Ministers. Sir Edward Grey tended to make a virtue of this necessity by his dictum that, in war, a Foreign Secretary could have no policy but to do what the soldiers wanted. The first lesson that had to be learnt by us amateurs in war was that this subservience to immediate military needs has its limits. One of our routines that August was to transmit to foreign governments the Admiralty notices of the requisitioning of warships under construction for them in British yards. Such requisitioning was a well-understood practice and was acquiesced in by the governments concerned. But among these messages was a curt notice to the government at Constantinople about the battleship which had become in Turkey the popular symbol of a new revolutionary nationalism. Fresh from the remote United States, I was the only member of the War Department who could have failed to realize the explosive possibilities of that notice, but I happened to be alone in the Department when the Admiralty draft arrived and the only initials on the "jacket" authorizing its dispatch are mine.

After that, a rule was made that not even routine telegrams

should be dispatched without the authority of, at least, the head of a department. But a later incident, which did not concern me personally, showed how easily the rule might break down. From the outbreak of war, official policy had been to refrain from invoking the Anglo-Japanese alliance. But, late one night, after the disaster of Coronel, the Cypher Department transmitted to Tokio an Admiralty message which they could not, they felt, take the responsibility of querying or delaying. It was a request for the co-operation of Japanese cruisers in the Pacific in the hunt for the *Scharnhorst* and *Gneisenau*. From that moment Japan became an active ally, with ultimate consequences in China and the Pacific, and in Anglo-American relations, which were to change history.

Probably, of course, even such monumental bricks dropped into the channel of history do not really change its course, but the dropper had better not lay that flattering unction to his soul. An admiral warned me, about this time, when he found me returning importantly to my office after dinner, that all the worst mistakes of the war had been made after 10 p.m.; and certainly, in war even more than in peace, the "drive" that fears to waste a minute often wastes more days than the red tape that enforces a regular procedure of decision and execution. And, as I was to see later, these harum-scarum methods of administration could be organized, by a temperamental Prime Minister, into a kind of systematic incoherence which reached its climax at Paris in 1919.

It is, indeed, extraordinary to remember how amateurish we all were in those days. Another dangerous expedient for rapid action was the circulation of Foreign Office telegrams, immediately on receipt, to other interested departments who were apt to act on them by the light of nature without waiting for an explanation. It was comparatively late in this first stage of the war that the proprietor of a great American newspaper, who had made friends with Sir Edward Grey on an earlier visit, came over to England again, heralded by a personal cable from our ambassador at Washington: "X sailed on s.s.———. Please look after him." As another American described the sequel to me, "they looked after him all right; they met him three miles out and had all the clothes off him before he knew what was happening." That incident did no harm; but, as in a mild way the American expert at the Foreign Office, I found the random witch-hunting of our multifarious "intelligence" agencies a constant anxiety. There was, in those days, a fascinating printed work of fiction, compiled and quite widely circulated by the Cable Censorship (which was, oddly enough, a section of the War Office), called the "Cable Censor's Handbook". In it I could find, in cold print, the names of many of my American friends, with fantastic deductions drawn, without any sort of inquiry, from their most trivial messages to their English and European correspondents. I think it was this same section which drew the attention of the Blockade authorities to the vast ramifications of a Spanish trading firm named Hijos.[1] Like the half-legendary medieval schoolmen who discussed how many angels could find standing room on the point of a needle, I used often to wonder how many non-existent spy rings could be balanced on the pen-nib of an amateur intelligence officer. Behind these amateurs worked the best real secret service in the world and a real military intelligence service which was almost as good; but they claimed no monopoly and exercised no control. Our national habit has been to allow every sub-department of war or police its own intelligence system, because we rightly calculate that the rioting of a dozen scratch beagle-packs on false scents does less harm than the single bloodhound of a secret police. But the beagles are trying to the nerves of anyone responsible for neighbouring hen-roosts.

2

In the autumn of 1915, I was transferred to the "Contraband" Department, which in due course blossomed into the Ministry of Blockade. That was thought to be a more suitable home for the peculiar activities in which I had become increasingly involved. For Sir Edward Grey had told me off a year earlier to act as liaison

[1] i.e., "Sons".

officer with the American Commission for Relief in Belgium and, in the eyes of an intermittently hostile Admiralty, intent on the "blockade", that meant that I had become Mr. Herbert Hoover's stooge.

The accusation was true enough, in the sense that I liked and trusted Hoover, that I admired the extraordinary organization built up by him and his associates, and that, once my government had adopted the policy of feeding a people behind the enemy lines, I took pride in seeing that policy effectively carried out. The story of the "C.R.B." has been so often told and so fully documented that I need only make two points about it here. The first is that, though I had infinite trouble in protecting Hoover from the interference of a multitude of minor scamperers in the rabbit warren of war administration, the Cabinet and the Foreign Office gave him consistent and understanding support. This seems worth saying because the published correspondence may give historians the impression that he was being constantly harried by extravagant demands from a ruthless Whitehall. That was, indeed, the impression that we intended to convey to the Germans, but the Americans to whom our demands were addressed hardly ever thought them unreasonable and, in fact, our language was often but a pale reflection of their own feelings. My second point is concerned with the question whether the policy of such relief could be justified in such a war. The scamperers never ceased to clamour that it was prolonging the war and this opinion has often been lightly repeated since. I am myself convinced that the relief operations had no material effect on the course of the war, one way or the other, except that, to some appreciable extent, it hampered the German army in Belgium and Northern France in their usual practice of official requisitions and private plunder. By the latter part of 1916 I was receiving from Hoover every fortnight a schedule of all complaints of requisitioning from all parts of Belgium, with notes of action taken upon them. I will not attempt to weigh the imponderables of "psychological warfare", but obviously what weight they had was in favour of the policy. On the other hand, the policy was too anomalous to be treated as a precedent. I never

thought it could be extended to Poland when that was tentatively
suggested by the Americans in 1916 and it could not possibly have
been repeated in the last war.

But, in retrospect, I feel that the real historical significance of
the whole story lay in its long-range effect on Anglo-American
relations. In order to bring this out, I must say something of
Herbert Hoover himself, even if that means breaking my rule
against writing about a living friend. In fact I shall be obliged to
break that rule often in my later chapters, wherever I find myself
writing of great public figures.

Hoover embodied all the best elements of American "isola-
tionism" – that is, of the temperamental tendency described by an
American wit in the phrase: "the foreign policy of the United
States is to have no foreign policy". He disliked all government
anyway: its claims to authority, it methods of administration and
its resultant pomposities and regulations. Later, in Washington in
1917, when he had just been appointed Food Administrator, he
confided to me that he doubted whether he could administer
a government department, since there was so much in such
administration that was repugnant to him, and all his abilities, he
felt, lay in the organization of voluntary effort. He was a member
of the Society of Friends – much more significantly so than I
realized in those early days, though, in those days, no one could
mistake his emotional humanity, his personal affectionateness and
his love of children. Even more significantly, perhaps, his recent
business experience had been in the successful operation of a free-
lance partnership of mining consultants in the development of
out-of-the-way mineral sources, neglected or mismanaged by
governments. He was temperamentally a free lance, and his very
soft heart and very hard head alike prompted an instinctive attitude to all governments which could be best summed up in the
words: "kindly get out of my way". There is no government
more calculated to arouse that instinct in such a man than the
British – except always the German. Hoover was too shy and
too sensitive to deal happily with Mr. Darcy and, unfortunately,
he made too little distinction between the honest buttoned-up

Darcies of the regular civil service and the scampering Darcies of the war-time rabbit warren.

It was with the scamperers that he and I collided in a Gilbertian – nay, rather, Learesque – episode in the winter of 1915–16. Two minor politicians and a chair-borne admiral on the outer fringes of Admiralty "intelligence", stumbling on a mare's nest, suddenly delated Hoover as a man with sinister German associations and myself as "an unpractical young idealist"; and demanded that relief shipments should be stopped pending a drastic investigation. The scrimmage became so heated that Sir Edward Grey felt obliged to appoint a kind of court of honour in the shape of a High Court judge, sitting in chambers. The result, of course, was to demolish the mare's nest, but the episode left a scar. It was not Hoover's first experience of a certain "no-nonsense" type of British naval officer, too common in those days, though now almost eradicated by the realism of two world wars – a type that the British public had come to treat as a joke, without realizing how easily, if allowed to escape from the home circle, it might become a dangerously bad joke. Nor was it to be his last. He has told in his memoirs of his youthful brush at Tientsin, during its siege by the Boxers, with a ram-you-damn-you captain on the China station and of his later encounter at Brussels in 1919 with that fine flower of naval Darcydom, "Rosy" Wemyss, who at the end of the war had surprisingly woken up to find himself First Sea Lord. These memories were to have at least a minor influence on future conflicts and misunderstandings. I was obliged, I remember, to tell this story to Austen Chamberlain after a Cabinet meeting, about the time of the Geneva Naval Conference in 1927, when he had confessed himself naïvely puzzled by Hoover's personal dislike of the British Admiralty.

Perhaps, too, another episode in the history of the C.R.B. had its influence on the future. In August 1916, Hoover had his culminating "show-down" with the Germans, over the protection of the harvest in the occupied areas. The show-down began, as usual, with a British ultimatum which Hoover took to Berlin. It looked as if, this time, we had overplayed our hand, for the German

General Staff refused flatly to entangle their commands in Northern France in the same network of restrictions that they had, they felt, been trapped into in Belgium. Instead, they proposed to stop all relief operations. At that point, Hoover, as he told me the story immediately afterwards, found himself one evening in private conversation with the General chiefly concerned, who had also been the officer responsible for the execution of Nurse Cavell. He complained bitterly to Hoover of the vilification he had suffered in the foreign press over that incident. He had merely done his duty as a German soldier and his action had been plainly justified by the laws of war. Hoover refused to comment, but suggested that world opinion would condemn at least as strongly, even if as unjustly, the starvation of thousands of Belgian and French children. The next day, to his surprise, the Germans reversed their decision and accepted his terms. The moral that he drew from that experience was that the one thing these "big, fat, retaliatory Germans" feared was the "brand of Cain" stamped on them by public opinion. It may not be wholly fanciful to give that anecdote its place in the curious history of the American doctrine of "non-recognition" – the belief in moral reprobation as an instrument of foreign policy – as it developed from Woodrow Wilson's use of it against a Mexican dictator in 1913 to Hoover's own use of it against Japan in 1932. I shall have to return, in Chapter x, to the later history of this doctrine as it has reappeared in the League of Nations and the United Nations.

3

During 1916, blockade diplomacy came to bulk larger in my work than Belgian relief. I visited Washington for a fortnight that Easter, to refresh personal contacts and correct my estimate of American tendencies. By that time, the main issue of British interference with trade between the United States and European neutrals had been settled – that is to say, the legal argument with the United States Government had ended in a deadlock, but a practical basis had been found upon which the most important interests of American manufacturers and traders could be recon-

ciled with the operations of the blockade. In that settlement I
had no hand; but a new phase was opening. In that phase,
controversy was to shift to the newer elaborations of British war
trade strategy, in the "Black List" and the Postal Censorship,
while the fresh prospect emerged of America's entry into the war
as an ally.

Reminiscences of our diplomacy at Washington in that period
have been sometimes written, notably by my friend Sir Arthur
Willert, in terms of "bringing America into the war". But that
was no part of British policy. The War Office and Admiralty were
inclined, indeed, to fight shy of the idea of American intervention,
even up to the last moment. Our policy, rightly or wrongly, was
no more than to keep the United States quiet and to secure her
grumbling acquiescence in the blockade. In that setting it is bad
history to write of our Embassy at Washington, as Sir Arthur
does, without so much as mentioning the name of Sir Richard
Crawford, its very able and very wise financial and economic
counsellor. For it was under his auspices that the "navicert"
system was invented, one of the few devices of the first war to be
revived almost unchanged in the second. Under that system,
amazingly enough, a British executive agency for the licensing of
American cargoes to Europe was set up on American soil and
operated by a foreign embassy not only under the nose of the
State and Commerce Departments, but with their tacit goodwill.

At another level, indeed, our policy had been concerned to
prevent American territory from being used as a base of enemy
operations; and for that purpose we had organized a brilliant
counter-espionage service, for which our diplomatic representatives could not, in the nature of things, accept responsibility. As
President Wilson developed his own peculiar brand of secret
diplomacy, out of sight of Congress and even of his own Cabinet,
this service, thanks to the presence in it of a very exceptional intelligence officer, Sir William Wiseman, became the natural
channel of communication with Colonel House, the President's
confidential agent. Of this semi-subterranean system of communications, which is the subject of Sir Arthur Willert's book, I am no

D

judge, for, on the only occasion when I touched the fringes of it, I showed myself far too clumsy at the game. But those who operated it were concerned rather to deter the President from inconvenient offers of mediation than to tempt him into active intervention. No legend is, in fact, more absurd than the one so popular in the United States between the wars, that America was inveigled into intervention in 1917 by a subtle apparatus of secret diplomacy.

However that may be, the time of my flying visit to Washington in 1916 marked the beginning of a new chapter. It was the Easter of the Irish rebellion, of whose repercussions on Anglo-American relations I need say only that it was as unwelcome to leaders of Irish-American opinion as it was to the British Government. It was also the Easter of the *Sussex* crisis, arising out of the torpedoing of a Channel steamer with Americans on board; and the President's message to Congress on that occasion brought the United States consciously to the very threshold of war. Indeed, one word from the President might have carried her across it. My strong impression at the time was that American opinion was then ready for war, though not as resolutely so as it was to be a year later. A year before, by contrast, at the time of the more famous *Lusitania* crisis, it had been wholly unready, split as it was between fervid pro-German, pro-Ally and neutralist factions. Now – as the head of a great hardware business described it to me, summarizing the reports of his salesmen throughout the continent – the contrasting colours on the American map had toned down to a uniform hue, a sort of drab acceptance of the inevitable. That acceptance was still compatible with a feeling expressed to me by a Western Senator in the quotation, "a curse on both your houses" – but it was enough to authorize an appeal to arms. That and later experience (as I shall have to suggest in discussing British re-armament in the 'thirties) has made me fancy that twelve months tends to be about the margin by which statesmen miss their chances. I offer that measure tentatively to the consideration of historians. That, anyway, was the impression that I brought home with me at the end of April 1916, with the conclusion that no necessary war measures that we might take would be seriously opposed by American opinion, provided always that we explained them frankly.

I must add a personal footnote to this summary of my flying visit. I was shocked to find myself, on my arrival, an object of suspicion to my colleagues at our Embassy. I was supposed to have been discrediting their reports ever since the beginning of the war and to have been murmuring criticisms of them into the multitudinous ears of Whitehall. This was pure myth. There had been criticisms, but I had taken no part in them and had, indeed, done my mild best to counteract them. True, I had never feared that the United States would seriously challenge our blockade and I had put my views on record in a general minute soon after the outbreak of war. That minute was, I think, reasonably prophetic and may have had some influence in leading the Foreign Office to take Sir Cecil Spring-Rice's subsequent warnings with more than a grain of salt; but I had not been consulted about those warnings for, until quite recently, I had had nothing to do with blockade policy. But the experience taught me how easily the *moral* of a foreign service may be spoilt by suspicions of ghost-voice interferences at home, and I may, later, have remembered that lesson too scrupulously.

At the time, I think my flying visit did a good deal to dissipate the myth in all minds but Spring-Rice's own. That most charming, but most sensitive, of men remained deeply suspicious of me because, I think, the situation reminded him of another situation in his own past. He had had, before I was eight years old, the same sort of youthful success at the Embassy at Washington as I had had in 1910–14. He had been the close friend of the young Theodore Roosevelt and, on the strength of this, he had visited Washington in 1904, with at least the encouragement of the Foreign Office, in an attempt to smoothe over the personal friction between Roosevelt and Sir Mortimer Durand. From then until he succeeded Bryce in 1913, he had been generally regarded as the predestined ambassador to the United States. Was I engaged on the same sort of mission now, and was I trying to build up the same kind of reputation – more prematurely and with, perhaps, an added touch of self-seeking of which he had always been innocent? These suspicions might have faded if I had been less clumsy and impatient – if the wine of war urgency had gone less to my head; as it was, they continued to spoil my relations with a very lovable man for whom I felt a genuine affection and whose work at Washington has always seemed to me to deserve more praise than it has received.

In the circumstances of the first two years of the war, the strength of an ambassador in Washington was to sit still. Those years saw the expulsion from the United States of an Austrian ambassador and German military attaché; by contrast, Spring-Rice's discretion served well to enhance the reputation of his country. His relations with the subterranean diplomacy to which I have already referred were a model of understanding tact. His reports to London were, no doubt, unduly alarmist, but there was, in truth, some real danger lest the blockade controversy might have developed on the lines which had culminated a century before in the war of 1812. President Wilson might easily have been tempted to emulate President Jefferson, the patron saint of the Democratic party, now once again in power after long years in the wilderness. Pro-Ally feeling, as its best representative, Mr. H. L. Stimson, has brought out in his memoirs, was still inspired in those years by old American doctrines of the laws of war and the rights of neutrals, and it would have been fatally easy to have turned it sour. Not until 1916 did it begin to take on the colour of a crusade against Prussianism. Discretion at such a time was no easy task for a romantic like Spring-Rice, who had sworn himself to the same crusade many years before and whom I had found in the corridors of the Foreign Office, on the night of the declaration of war, murmuring to himself verses from the imprecatory psalms – "their words are softer than butter, but war is in their hearts". Self-suppression – suppression both of his public feelings and of his personal genius for friendship – told on his nerves and wore down a health which had never been robust; but, in the spring of 1917 he could have fairly claimed, if his modesty had ever thought of doing so, that he had enabled America to enter the war deliberately, of her own motion, on a united impulse, and in a cause which she had made her own. For the myth that she was swept into it on a tide of propaganda, or to serve the interests of bankers and munition makers, was a later growth: no such myth clouded, as a little injudicious propaganda might so easily have clouded it, the *moral* of her people or of her army in the days of actual war.

If our diplomacy in those years had refrained too scupulously from making any direct appeal to American public opinion, the fault lay with London, not with Spring-Rice. Even if he had had Bryce's talent for academic propaganda, there was no scope for it then. Much of convinced pro-Ally opinion, from Spring-Rice's best friend, Theodore Roosevelt, downwards, was too distinctly Republican, too indiscreet, and too contemptuous of the President, for an ambassador to be able safely to accept its aid or to supply it with texts of his own to preach from. But perhaps some of the voluminous legal notes on the blockade, which had been drafted in London, could have been more human and more readable. We did make at least one not unsuccessful attempt at a more human appeal in 1916: in the "Black List" note of October, which I am glad to remember I had some hand in drafting. But we need not, perhaps, have waited so long.

I had another assignment in 1916, the secretaryship of a Foreign Office Committee on the administration of British international commercial relations after the war. I had better reserve this for a later chapter, when I come to discuss certain aspects of foreign policy between wars.

4

In April 1917 I returned to Washington, rather reluctantly for the reasons I have indicated. I went as a member of the Balfour Mission and stayed behind for a year as representative of the Ministry of Blockade attached to the Embassy.

The Mission had its humours. At its outset, the special train that should have taken us to Stranraer got no farther than Dumfries, where we spent some twenty hours in the Station Hotel, trying to screen our Chief's conspicuous figure from prying eyes. It was like him to make nonsense of our precautions by confessing, on our departure, that he had given his autograph to the boot boy. On the other side of the Atlantic, I became at once blackly discredited with my colleagues; for General Bridges and Admiral De Chair took my sage advice that they had better enter the United States in mufti, only to wake up to the vision of the American Chiefs of Staff pacing the single platform of the tiny frontier station in full uniform, showing up in the early dawn as startlingly as blue jays against the grey Maine scrub. No miscalculation could, of course, have been more absurd than to conceal the panoply of war from a people whose main feeling at that moment was that, after so many hesitations, they knew at last where they were.

In speaking of the diplomacy of my year in Washington, I want to confine myself to my own blockade work, but I must set it against a curious background of incoherent government. Perhaps that is too sweeping a condemnation; I can best describe what I mean by saying that I then first began to feel in my work that I was a member of a driverless team of horses. It was quite a different feeling from the lethargic coachmanship which many of us had criticized in Asquith's government; now there was plenty of whip behind us, and even more confused cries and adjurations, but there seemed to be no hand on the reins. Of the two governments with whom I was concerned, this was less true of the American than of the British. There was at least an intermittent hand on the American reins – the President's own, when he found time to take them. His intervals of inattention cost the world much in the long run; for instance, he left the financial rein to his son-in-law and Secretary of the Treasury, McAdoo, in whose conduct one could never help suspecting a spice of sheer Irish ill-will; and it is arguable that this negligence gave the post-war problem of inter-Allied debts its peculiarly intractable form. But in the conduct of the war itself these intervals of inattention were brief enough to do little serious harm. By contrast, it seemed to me that Lloyd George neither held the reins himself nor allowed anyone else to hold them; he could use only the whip and, occasionally, the brake.

The first sign to me of this detached style of driving came when Balfour had hardly left for home. By that time, it was clear that a new ambassador must be appointed who could take control of the multifarious British technical missions in Washington and New York, as Lord Reading was to do a year later. Spring-Rice himself wished to take this opportunity of retiring; Balfour refrained from taking him home with him, as his adviser on American affairs, only with the intention of arranging a still more dignified exit for him and avoiding an interregnum. But before he got home Lloyd George, without consulting him, appointed as High Commissioner a man who could not reasonably take the position of ambassador, yet whose function in relation to the ambassador was left quite undefined. Lord Northcliffe, in fact, did well enough in charge of the technical missions, at least for some six months; for such Anglo-American teams can usually be trusted to drive themselves for the ordinary purposes of the road. He pretended to no qualifications as a business administrator and he disclaimed any responsibility for my blockade work; in my few contacts with him, I liked him and found him friendly. But I hardly think it would be unfair to say that the result was to leave the representation of British power and policy in the hands of two political nonentities in Washington and New York, one prematurely aged and one a boy who had never grown up, while preparations for eventual peace went on in the subterranean whispering galleries of Colonel House. Normal political communications ceased between the two governments, and it was small wonder that any echoes of Balfour's warnings about European nationalism and the "secret treaties" should have died away in the insulated recesses of the White House.

Against the background of that monumental blunder, my own little difficulties were unimportant; but they were ominous. My instructions were to induce the United States Government to present to European neutrals – especially to the three Scandinavian countries and the Netherlands – the sheer alternatives of either

ceasing all trade with Germany or ceasing all trade with the United
States. The response of the United States Government was to
prohibit all exports to the neutrals and then to establish a War
Trade Board to advise the President upon what conditions and to
what extent the prohibition might be relaxed. No body could
have been friendlier than this Board; they admitted me and my
French colleague to their deliberations and treated me frankly as
one of themselves; but, looking back, I find it difficult to imagine
what we could have talked about in all our long sessions from
May to September. For the diplomatic deadlock was complete;
the neutrals were, for all practical purposes, in a blockade lock-up,
but no one was willing to tell them how they could escape, while
they, on their side, were not eager to buy their way out, doubting
whether their jailers were in earnest. The State Department could
not bring itself to demand from them complete renunciation
of their trade with Germany; and on one occasion, when that
demand was made brusquely to Nansen, the Norwegian Ambassador, by Hoover's representative on the War Trade Board, the
State Department rapped him smartly over the knuckles. Yet I
was not authorized to agree to any lesser demand. The State
Department grew increasingly restive and its Assistant Secretary
complained (so Sir Richard Crawford informed me) that I
represented the "Robert Cecil school of arrogant diplomacy".
Again, the shade of Mr. Darcy! So the neutrals received no
American supplies, but their exports of domestic produce (such as
Norwegian chrome) continued (for all we knew) to find their
way to Germany.

At this point, a new factor entered mysteriously into the
negotiations. One day, the same Assistant Secretary told Crawford
that "Percy is evidently not in the confidence of his government".
It took me some time to discover what this meant. It eventually
appeared that Lord Reading, visiting the President on a special
financial mission, had handed to him a sealed envelope entrusted to
him by Lloyd George, the contents of which he did not know. On
further inquiry, it appeared that the envelope contained a secret
Admiralty memorandum, enlarging on the danger of driving

Norway into war with Germany and thus risking a seizure of Norwegian ports by the Germany navy. That was an obvious risk which, perhaps, the Foreign Office had too lightly discounted and which, probably, the Admiralty had taken too seriously. But the two estimates had never been compared in any responsible discussion. I subsequently found that Robert Cecil, then Minister of Blockade, had heard vaguely of the memorandum, but had never seen it. It was thus that the Lloyd George War Cabinet worked.

Indeed, I doubt whether the State Department ever saw it. I certainly never did. It remained, quite unnecessarily, part of the "top-secret" dossier of the War Cabinet and the White House, second-hand accounts of which leaked out to fog the air of ordinary international business. In this fog, it was hopeless to expect from the United States Government any reasonable solution of the deadlock; what seemed more likely was that the State Department or the White House might be scared into some irrational intervention. At the end of September, I took the only course that seemed possible: disobeying my instructions, I went privately to Nansen and asked him to take the initiative in proposing a compromise. The result was a series of agreements with the neutrals which seemed to me not unsatisfactory; but they evoked passionate protests from London, and not least from the Admiralty itself.

After that, I relapsed increasingly into odd jobs on the diplomatic fringes of the technical missions. I need record only two incidents of that winter.

Northcliffe had gone home on leave, after experimenting with a speech-making tour in the Middle West. I had heard little of the tour, but it seemed that, without any flagrant indiscretions, he had trodden on just a sufficient number of sensitive toes to confirm the wisdom of Spring-Rice's indomitable silence. Sufficient, too – so an excited group of friends came to assure me one evening – to make it highly undesirable for him to return. On that impulse I wrote to him personally, advising him that he had done his work and had better not challenge enmities by coming back. I do not suppose this letter had much to do with his decision to stay in England, but he greeted me in a London drawing-room the following spring with "you see, I took your advice".

At Christmas, I myself paid a flying visit to London to confer with the Foreign Office. Before I was due back, the Ministry of Shipping sent for me to tell me that there was less than a month's (the actual estimate was, I think, a fortnight's) reserve of grain in the country, and that I must take the next boat back and urge Hoover personally to action. What with reports of submarines and Atlantic storms, the next boat took eleven days to reach New York, where I found Hoover and the head of the Shipping Board a little sceptical of my news, but anyway powerless, for the railroad gateways through the Alleghanies were frozen up and no traffic was moving to the coast. The ice-breakers were busy in New York harbour, and at Washington that night the thermometer marked forty-five degrees of frost, with no apparent prospect of a thaw. But the thaw came next day. That led to some discussions with Hoover about grain and meat shipments and indirectly to my participation in one of the queerest episodes of American war trade policy: the seizure of the Dutch merchant fleet in United States ports. But it was clear to me that I was becoming something of a fifth wheel to the Anglo-American diplomatic coach, and the Foreign Office agreed that I should come home after Easter when Lord Reading took over the Embassy.

My voyage home in the *Aquitania*, with 6,000 American troops on board, during the latter days of the German spring offensive in France, marked, in a sense, the end of the war for me. From then to the Armistice, I was to work in the "Political Intelligence" department of the Foreign Office, whose main business was not war, but preparation for peace. For me, those months were mainly an introduction to the Peace Conference. They were also an introduction to marriage, which I achieved at the beginning of December. That is another story; though, like most happy men, I think of it as the adventure in life where I have least failed, though the credit for success does not belong to me.

Before, however, I leave these war years, I must note one

memory of the Washington spring and summer of 1917. A
Congressman from California, whom I had known in the "House
of Truth" (where I had taken up my residence again) as an illumi-
nating, if cynical, commentator on political life and manners, had
the idea of organizing weekly breakfast parties, preceded by a
mildly strenuous course of "physical jerks" in his large garden.
The regular attenders, of whom I was one, were mostly a mixed
bag of Cabinet Ministers and other "senior executives". We
talked no politics, but some of us got to know each other in our
shirt-sleeves. We must have broken our instructor's heart, for
most of us were middle aged and of sedentary habit; our only
reasonably athletic member, it is sad to remember, was the
Assistant Secretary of the Navy, Franklin Roosevelt.

One other impression may be worth recording of my last days
in Washington. I had long had a number of contacts with American Jewry and I now felt overwhelmed by the enthusiasm with
which it greeted the Balfour Declaration. It was my first taste of
the many popular exuberances which were to be so tragically disappointed by the realities of post-war politics. My own relation to
Zionism had been peculiar. I believed in it as a live, and probably
irresistible, political force and, in the exchange of Cabinet memoranda on the subject early in the war, which I had read in the
Foreign Office, my sympathies had been with Herbert Samuel
rather than with Edwin Montagu. But I doubted whether any
form of Jewish Palestine could find a place in a stable international
system; I thought it more probable that, in the words of Zechariah,
a Zionist Jerusalem would prove a "burdensome stone for all
people". I had therefore taken as little part in the preliminaries of
the Balfour Declaration as I could; indeed, I think my only part in
them had been to arrange that breakfast meeting between Balfour
and my friend Justice Brandeis, where I suspect (for I was not
present) the formula of the "national home" was first adumbrated.
But I could not help sunning myself in the jubilation of my friends,
and perhaps I cannot be much blamed for letting the sun get a
little in my eyes. It was not the only time in the next twelve months
that I was to allow peace dreams to dazzle me out of sober sense.

CHAPTER IV

Peace-making 1918-19

I

So much has been written about the Peace Conference of 1919 that I can hardly hope to add any material facts to the record. What I can, perhaps, add is a newish point of view. My own part in the Conference was undistinguished enough. In my first two months in Paris, from January to March, I was concerned almost exclusively with the drafting of the Covenant of The League of Nations. I was there as Lord Robert Cecil's assistant for that purpose and, when the inter-Allied Commission on the League was formed, I became one of its three secretaries – American, British and French. I enjoyed these two months. I had a definite job and it ended in a definite achievement – whether wise or unwise is another matter. I was only too conscious that the League was being born into a household which already threatened to become a "broken home"; but the confusion and divided counsels of that household had, as yet, not degenerated into chaos. Soon after the Commission had reported the first text of the Covenant to the Conference, I resigned from the Foreign Office in order to stand for Parliament. At the beginning of May, while I was still licking my wounds after an ignominious by-election defeat, I returned to Paris for another two months as temporary assistant private secretary to the Foreign Secretary, Mr. Balfour. This last anomalous addendum to my foreign service was, I think, the most exasperating episode of my life. Chaos had come. To be actively concerned in a scrimmage may be, at least, exciting; but to watch one from a private secretary's desk is a weariness of the spirit. "At this Conference," my chief said to me one day, "all important business is transacted in the intervals of other business", and that still seems to me the best comment on this early experiment in what has since come to be known as "top-level" diplomacy.

In all this, what I call my newish point of view is that the Anglo-American aspect of this incoherence was much more disastrous than the European aspect, though I should be afraid to claim that I realized the full extent of the disaster at the time. Looking back, I seem, indeed, to have lived, consciously enough, under its shadow through all these six months – from December 1918, when honeymoon days were disturbed by the intolerable discord between the vulgarities of the General Election and the cold crackle of pontifical wireless messages punctuating President Wilson's voyage across the Atlantic, until June 1919, when I could not bring myself to attend the signing of the Peace Treaty with Germany at Versailles. But I think that, in all this time, I was actually more sensitive to the bad tone of public utterances than to material blunders in policy. It has, indeed, always seemed to me more reasonable to judge politicians by their words than by their acts. Except under a real dictatorship, personal responsibility for acts of government can seldom be brought home to a single individual actor; but every man has a right to be taken at his own word. But I must now try to reconstruct, in retrospect, our blunders in Anglo-American policy in terms of action, instead of merely in terms of language and attitude.

2

British policy at the Conference should have had two major aims: the peace settlement proper and the settlement of Anglo-American relations. The two aims were, of course, intimately related to one another; but the second was by far the more important. The Europe represented at the Conference, without Russia or Germany, and with the Austro-Hungarian empire already split, *de facto*, into its succession states, no longer contained the elements either of a stable balance of power or of a genuinely co-operative league of nations; Western Asia between the Bosporus and the Persian Gulf was in even worse case; in Eastern

Asia, Japanese ambition and Chinese anarchy were big with the threat of future war. The construction of any new family of nations worthy of the name must depend in the long run, on nothing less than an alliance between the English-speaking nations of the British Commonwealth and the United States. To all who knew the United States, the prospect of her entry into such an alliance might seem infinitely remote; but, since it was essential, it must be the constant aim of British policy. In politics, it is folly to mistake a dream for present fact; but it is wisdom in a statesman to dream thirty years ahead; and this particular dream was to come true well within thirty years after 1919. The tragic question is whether in 1919 we did not miss the opportunity of setting the United States on the road towards its realization, without having to pay the price of a second world war. I think we did; indeed, almost every action we took and, still more, almost every word we spoke from November 1918 onwards seemed to be calculated to render us, in American eyes, less desirable as an ally or even as a friend.

Of course, we were not batting on an easy wicket. To begin with, there were two crude factors in American feeling about Britain, of which we took too little account. One was jealousy, and even fear, of the dominant position which the war had given us; the other was pride in the decisive contribution which Americans felt they had made towards the Allied victory. During the first half of the war, a common legend among would-be hard-headed American foreign correspondents abroad and editorial writers at home had been that Britain was leaving France to do the fighting for her, in the hope that she would be strong enough at the end of the war to impose her own kind of peace, not only on her enemies, but also on her exhausted allies. Now, on the eve of the Armistice, one of the best of these correspondents, who had done much latterly to dissipate the legend, confessed to me, rather naïvely, how much he was disturbed by the thought of the overwhelming preponderance of Britain in the post-war world, especially in naval power. In 1917 another, and much shrewder, American friend had told me prophetically that he hoped the war would not end quickly for, if it did, the tougher element in American public opinion would easily assume that the mere appearance of an American army in the field had been enough to ensure victory. That prophecy came true, and the assumption is oddly reflected even in the first volume of Mr. Hoover's memoirs, written in the 1920s, where he refers, in passing, to the transformation scene in the summer of 1918 as having been due to "Pershing's victories". These two impulses of jealousy and pride could combine, only too easily, in the exasperated feeling that all America's efforts and sacrifices were being thrown into the crucible of British policy to forge the instruments of British world power.

This, for the tougher American, was the sting of Article 10 of the Covenant of the League of Nations, the guarantee of mutual defence against aggression. The Senator who told me with Puckish delight how, in a press statement, he had stigmatized that Article as a device for pledging American arms "to the defence of the territories of the *Kaiser-i-Hind*" may have allowed his instinct for a catchword to run away with him; but, after all, if he had lived until 1943, he might have claimed that his catchword had been a prophecy. Among the Great Powers, Britain in 1919 was, indeed, to all appearances the only beneficiary of the war, the only victor who had given a multitude of new hostages to fortune. No country stood to gain more from a general guarantee of her possessions.

Moreover, how could Americans, who looked at British power through such a magnifying glass, fail to conclude that Britain had been the promoter of all those "secret treaties" which so naturally offended American opinion? How could they imagine the almost anguished reluctance of the British Foreign Office in the spring of 1915 to buy Italy's alliance at the price of concessions to her in the Adriatic, or how a protesting Cabinet had been almost bullied into paying the price by Kitchener's insistence that, at any cost, the Italian army must be brought into the field? Still more, how could they imagine that Britain, the ally of Japan, was bitterly opposed to Japan's policy of encroachment in China and, that the Foreign

Office, foreseeing it, would gladly have kept Japan out of the war? And, after all, in the Middle East, was it not true that Britain had, indeed, been herself the chief author of a net-work of half-contradictory engagements, designed to reconcile the establishment of an Arab empire, not only with the creation of a Jewish "national home" in Palestine, but also with French ambitions in Syria? Had not some British civil servants already found it difficult to explain to puzzled American experts, on the eve of the Peace Conference, why a Wahabi army, munitioned by the Government of India, was attacking a Mecca equipped with arms supplied by the Government in London? The tougher sort of Americans might, indeed, have been content to shrug their shoulders over all this for, as I have already suggested, they had, from of old, no high opinion of Mr. Darcy's wisdom, or of his nerve in time of danger; and they had no intention anyway of guaranteeing even an impeccable distribution of the territories of the old Austro-Hungarian and Turkish empires, nor were they yet quite awakened to Japan's threat to the balance of power in the Pacific. But in the United States – and in Britain, for that matter – toughness is never at ease with itself unless it can speak the language of morality and, in the language of morality, as spoken in the America of Woodrow Wilson, the secret treaties naturally took on a darker colour.

As an illustration, it is worth quoting the speech of another Senatorial aquaintance of mine, Norris of Nebraska, a "progressive" Republican representing the mingled toughness and moralism of the Middle West, who changed in a few months from an ardent believer in the idea of a League of Nations to a bitter opponent of the whole Peace Treaty. He had, he said in 1920, thought that "Article 10 was almost damnable"; but he had been prepared to swallow it. But

"When I discovered that these same men, who had talked eloquently here to us, had in their pockets secret treaties when they did it; when I discovered that they pulled out those secret treaties at the peace table, in contravention and in contradiction

to every agreement that they made when we entered the peace
conference; when I saw that they were demanding that these
secret treaties be legalized; and, more than all, when I saw our
own President lie down and give in and submit to the disgrace,
the dishonour, the crime and the sin of that treaty, then I said:
'Great God! I don't believe I want to have any dealings with
any of you people. I am suspicious of you all the way through.
You are dishonest. You have not been fair with us or with the
world. You have been wicked. You have concluded to act here
just the same as you were acting in barbarous days, after pro-
claiming to us, and after we believed that you were in earnest
and fighting for democracy to build a peace, a world peace, a
league of nations that would bring peace and happiness for ever
to a suffering people.' "

This speech was almost infinitely remote from the facts. Out-
raged virtue is never a fair witness; but the virtue was genuine
enough, and so was the outrage. Britain had not indeed, been the
chief promoter of the secret treaties, nor, by the ordinary standards
of diplomacy, could she be fairly accused of having concealed
them from the Government of the United States; but her public
men had far outdistanced their allies in using the loftiest language
to describe their war aims, and they could not complain if
literally-minded Americans took them at their word. Even so, on
the merits of the territorial settlement eventually reached, in spite
of these prior commitments, Britain had quite a good case; but the
case had to be made and defended, and her statesmen failed to
make and defend it. They were unconscious of the breakdown of
real diplomatic relations with the United States which had been
increasingly apparent ever since President Wilson had entered the
White House six years before; and they seemed content to let their
case go by default. The mission entrusted to Sir Edward Grey
as special ambassador at Washington was hardly more than a
"gesture", to use the ill-omened word which was then beginning
to come into fashion, and, as it turned out, a deplorably miscalculated one.

E

Anyway, given the tone of British policy, both at home and at Paris, there was not much that British diplomacy could do at Washington to enhance British moral prestige. Diplomacy there, even of the popular kind, must continue to be, as it was in Bryce's day, a long range investment; it might have prevented the deepening rift between the two countries which followed the rejection by Congress of the Peace Treaties, but it could not have much affected the fate of the Treaties themselves. What might have conceivably affected their fate would have been a fundamentally different policy in London and Paris on two crucial points: the drafting of the Covenant and the restoration of the economic life of Europe.

3

Mr. H. L. Stimson has summed up in his memoirs what he and Mr. Elihu Root thought at the time should have been, from the American point of view, the form of the Covenant. In contrast to President Wilson's idea of "a full-fledged Covenant, complete in all its parts, and wholly up to date in its assertion of the joint responsibility of all the nations for the maintenance of peace", he wrote:

> "The League should have been a much more general charter, and it should be permitted to grow and develop gradually, adding to its formal obligations only as the genuine sentiment of the nations permitted. In this fashion, they believed, the slowly growing spirit of international responsibility might be fostered, unchecked by the disillusionment of broken pledges. To them the central requirement was for a constantly available international meeting ground. The ancient pride of sovereign nations could not be ended in a day, but if international discussion could become a regular habit, and if the United States, particularly, could learn to consider herself a participant in the world's problems, then the resort to war might not become necessary."[1]

[1] Stimson and Bundy, *On Active Service in Peace and War*, pp. 102–3.

This view was shared by Mr. Hoover at the time, and it probably represented a strong enough body of opinion in the United States, if not to have secured the ratification of such a modified Covenant by Congress in 1920, at least to have robbed rejection of its bitterness and to have made it relatively easy for Hoover and Stimson to have brought the United States into a League of that kind when they became President and Secretary of State in 1929. The tragedy is that this was, with one substantial difference, the view also of the British drafters of the Covenant before the Conference; and, even after the Conference, one at least of them thought that they had put it into practice. I hardly know whether to laugh or cry when I read some words I wrote in the late summer of 1919:

> "There were two alternatives before them (the leaders at Paris) – either to create a half-legalist, half-militarist system of compulsory arbitration and international police armament, or to perpetuate, in new soil and, so far as possible, in a new atmosphere, the natural growth of international co-operation and consultation as represented in the Paris Conference itself. The first alternative was probably far the most popular and the most widely advertised, but its rejection was the greatest, perhaps the only great, stroke of statesmanship achieved by British and American influence at Paris."

But, as I have said, there was one substantial difference between the official British and the educated American view: the question of some sort of guarantee of the settlement. There was much to justify the Stimson–Root–Hoover view of what should have been done at Paris; there was something to justify my own view of what had actually been done there. There could hardly be a better instance of how international like-mindedness may be distorted into conflict, and of the chief function of diplomacy in making like-mindedness conscious of itself. But the stumbling-block of Article 10 remained.

I was, I believe, the author of the first tentative draft of the Covenant in the Foreign Office in November 1918. That draft contained Article 10, but almost unthinkingly. To an Englishman, brought up on history, it was almost a matter of course to reproduce Pitt's idea, adumbrated in 1805, of an eventual peace between the Powers of Europe

> "by which their respective rights and possessions . . . shall be fixed and recognized; and they shall all bind themselves mutually to protect and support each other against any attempt to infringe them."

It was on the other hand, almost a matter of course, too, to regard any such obligation as dependent upon the character of the peace settlement, and to withdraw from it, as Castlereagh had tended to do after the Congress of Vienna, if, and in so far as, the settlement was not such as to deserve a British guarantee. I do not think I should have included such an article in the draft if I had foreseen that the first text of the Covenant would be settled in advance of the rest of the Peace Treaty and that the Allies would thus commit themselves to buy a pig in a poke. It is, in fact, extraordinary to remember how flatly ignorant some of the chief authors of the Covenant were about the nature of the pig. The Wilson of the Fourteen Points, for instance, was amazed to be told by one of his experts on his voyage to Europe that the new Czecho-Slovak State must contain a large German minority. "Mazaryk never told me that."

Moreover, in the context of this early draft, Article 10 was intended as little but a general introduction to the only concrete obligation assumed by the members of the League: that of abstention from all commercial intercourse with an aggressor who had failed to submit his dispute to the procedure of conciliation laid down in the Covenant. That obligation was a modest one, and one not, in itself, unacceptable to American opinion, as the later unfortunate history of American "Neutrality" Acts invertedly proved. Nevertheless, I am inclined to think now that this idea of general boycott as the penalty for refusal to conciliate, though hardly criticized at the time, was a worse blunder even than Article 10. It reflected the quite exaggerated value attached by Englishmen in those days to blockade, as a weapon of war, as the result of their concentration, over four hectic years, on building up an elaborate world-wide machinery to make blockade effective; and it accustomed a whole generation of Englishmen to the illusion that international lawlessness could, in the last resort, be prevented or repressed by something less costly than military intervention. It also ignored the fact that to Americans the blockade of Germany had been primarily a food blockade, and it therefore conflicted violently with Hoover's ingrained horror of starvation as a weapon of war.

Anyway, this draft of mine, lavishly corrected and expanded for the better, was the one brought by the British delegation to Paris, where, after fusion with a not dissimilar American document, it became, as the "Hurst-Miller" draft, the basis of discussion by the Inter-Allied Commission. Later, when the Commission came (in English parliamentary language) to "Report" stage, Lord Robert Cecil proposed the elimination of Article 10, as superfluous, meaningless and misleading. He found himself in a minority of one. President Wilson went so far as to say that it was this Article, more than all others, which represented the desires of "the plain people of the United States". When Cecil retorted: "Yes, but do any of us really mean it?", my American colleague threw across the secretaries' table to me a note: "Thank God for this man"; but Orlando replied that it was valuable as a general assurance of good intentions, and that seemed to represent the views of all the European delegates. Yet, with whatever reluctance, they would have followed Wilson if he had supported Cecil. In the end, though not at the beginning, Article 10 was his article and his alone.

This has always seemed to me to have been, so to speak, the symbolic moment at which Britain and the United States missed the chance of collaboration in the maintenance of peace and, with it, the only chance of any secure settlement. The two nations jointly did represent a different conception of the way to maintain peace from that traditional in continental nations: a conception of collaboration and, if necessary, progressive change, against a background of acknowledged but uncodified law, in contrast to conservative contentment with an armed *status quo* or radical ambition disguised under the ambiguous name of nationalism. As soon as the chance of defining and developing that conception was missed, Americans relapsed into the fatal habit of regarding Britain as inextricably part of the European system, to be included in the blanket description of "Eur Ope", an irredeemable tangle of national hates, jealousies and suspicions. That was a popular American language with which one had long been familiar; but it was the tragedy of the inter-war period that this language became the idiom of really educated Americans and even of experienced American diplomatists, until, in the Hoare–Laval crisis at the end of 1935, an old friend from the State Department could find nothing to say to me about the Abyssinian problem except an exasperated comment on the inability of "Europe" to settle its problems without war.

4

There had, however, been an earlier symbolic moment for me of the same kind: a November evening in Whitehall when Cecil told me that Lloyd George had summarily vetoed his project of visiting Clemenceau in Paris, to agree on the establishment of some form of Economic Council during the transition from war to peace. It is, no doubt, dangerous to attach too much importance to a single incident recollected at a distance of nearly forty years; but I do think that this occurrence epitomized several attitudes on one side or the other which postponed the establishment of a Supreme Economic Council for nearly four months and went far, in the interim, to wreck the chances of cordial Anglo-American co-operation in just the field where it would have been easiest: in the practical tasks of reconstruction. The chief of these attitudes were: Lloyd George's desire to keep in his own hands all possible bargaining counters which might prevent Wilson from, so to speak, running away with the Peace Conference; Hoover's reluctance to subordinate American economic interests and humanitarian impulses to international controls which might be

biased by European needs and prejudices; and the almost patho-
logical inability of both Wilson and Lloyd George to confine
their freedom of action within the limits of any regular administrative procedures.

For years trade between nations had been carried on within
limits laid down by international agreements and administered by
internationally recognized authorities; the transport of goods by
sea had been regulated by allocations of tonnage made by an inter-
allied Commission; and, though since 1917 the responsibility for
enforcing the blockade had, in large measure, passed from the
Allied navies to American customs officers, those officers, no less
than the navies, were operating under the authority of the
established international agreements and controls. In these circumstances a heedless disintegration of agreements and controls, such
as began almost immediately after the Armistice, must tend to
restore, not freedom of trade, but irresponsible action by individual governments. Moreover, if such a disbandment of international administration restored freedom to the United States to
modify its export policies in the interests of European reconstruction, it must, in almost the same measure, restore to each of the
Allied navies discretion to arrest goods in transit as a precaution
against the resurgence of a still possibly war-like Germany. And,
in fact, that is what happened. The United States demanded from
European neutrals the execution of war contracts for food supplies
at war prices in order to protect the quite legitimate interests of
American farmers; the British Government restricted the movements of German fishermen in the equally legitimate interests of
the British taxpayer, in order to unload on German consumers the
accumulated stocks of Norwegian herrings which they had
bought up during the war; Lloyd George thought that he had
commissioned Hoover to feed the starving in Europe, without
realizing that he had lost the means of giving corresponding
orders to the Allied navies – and so on. The continuance of the
blockade after the Armistice has been often bitterly attacked and
sometimes rather ineffectively defended or denied; but no commentators seem to me to have realized to what extent it was the

half-unintentional effect of pure administrative muddle. It was in the atmosphere of that muddle, where those responsible for the execution of conflicting or ill-adjusted policies had no regular opportunity of discussing and adapting them with their opposite numbers of other nations across a table, that, for four fatal months, some of the best of Americans formed the opinions about European politics which were to decide Anglo-American relations for the next twenty years.

If these were my thoughts at the time, they can, no doubt, be partly discounted as the thoughts of a civil servant to whom administrative incoherence is the worst of political vices. This prejudice has, I suppose, also been a little accentuated by a sneaking sense of guilt. I ought to have played an active part in these things, and I was, in fact, a mere spectator, almost a deserter. I knew the United States politically as few Englishmen did; I had worked for years with Hoover; for some months before the Armistice, I had been studying the problem of transitional trade relations after the war as one of a group of civil servants; and in a minor way I had been one of the authors of the League Covenant. My experience might have fitted me for some modest employment in this field of lost opportunities and, if I had been through the mill of such employment, I might not now be writing quite so critically. As it was, I tore up my civil service qualifications, such as they were, in order to stand for Parliament, while these issues were still in the balance. I like to remember that my last act as a civil servant was to write a memorandum for Cecil, proposing a drastic fining down of the Covenant in the further consideration of it then about to begin in Paris; but I am afraid my proposals were, at that stage, politically impossible and represented little more than a suicide's confession of error, *in articulo mortis*.

Yet, after making all these discounts, it still seems to me that these early confusions proved, in the long run, even more disastrous than the Reparations madness in which the Conference was to end. Or, at any rate, the confusions led inescapably to the madness. In the time-honoured phrase, "a just and lasting peace", the second adjective is the important one, and only in its light has the first any meaning. Theoretically, at least, a lasting peace may be imposed on a rebel against civilization by the method of retributive justice; but, in that case, the sentence must be, not merely announced by a judge, but enforced by a sustained exercise of executive power. A just sentence which those imposing it are either unwilling or unable to enforce for the necessary period is a frivolity; and it was to that frivolity that the England of the General Election of 1918 committed herself. She might have brought herself to face the brief exertion of "hanging the Kaiser"; she certainly was in no mood to make the protracted effort required to keep an independent Germany disarmed – an effort which, a century before, had proved to be beyond the strength and intelligence of Napoleon. The futility, from this point of view, of the "military" clauses of the Peace Treaty was obvious enough, at the time, to many "right wing" Englishmen who were no advocates of leniency to a Germany whom they still regarded as a dangerous enemy. What was, unfortunately, not so obvious to them was that the Reparations clauses must prove even more unenforceable, at any rate by any methods which the creditor nations could concert in a world of broken exchanges, or by any sanctions they were likely to impose on a recalcitrant debtor. In these circumstances a lasting peace could be secured only by the method of distributive justice: by the reconstruction of an international society on a plan which, however hotly resented at first by a defeated Germany, would win gradual and increasing acceptance by the practical benefits which it would confer on its members. It was on that policy of reconstruction that the leaders of England turned their back even before the General Election; it was on a Europe apparently incapable of reconstruction that America began to turn her back, even before the Conference met.

5

To all this criticism, let me append a confession. If a civil servant is to feel sure that he is wiser than parliamentary politicians, he had better not stand for Parliament himself. The by-election which I fought in Central Hull in March 1919 is the episode in my life which I least like to remember. Not because I made, in many ways, a public ass of myself, for other raw candidates have done as badly before and since. Still less because I lost, spectacularly, a seat which, on paper, I ought to have won easily; for, even if I had been an impeccable candidate, I was fighting at a serious disadvantage. In four years of war, I had never worn a uniform or heard a shot fired in anger; yet here I was, advocating a renewal of conscription, under the Military Service Bill, introduced into the House of Commons at the end of February – and that at a moment when the public temper was accurately expressed to me by a decent young soldier on leave from France: "I would vote for the devil himself if he promised to get me demobilized." If that had been all, I might have taken some pride in defeat; for I was, at least defending the truth that a New Europe could not be built by a nation which had disarmed itself prematurely and was content to chatter about "self-determination". But my defence was marred by puerilities which I would gladly forget.

I distrusted Lloyd George, for the reasons I have already indicated; but I did my best to make my audiences believe that I stood as his whole-hearted supporter. I had, as I have explained, held aloof from Zionism; but I represented myself to the large Jewish element in the constituency as having been very much on the inside of the discussions which had led to the Balfour Declaration. These are the two chief dishonesties that I remember; but, in general, I think that I struck most of the false notes which had so jarred on my civil servant ears in the general election only three months before. After such a shaky solo performance, I have small right to criticize the discords of the earlier orchestra.

CHAPTER V

Miscellaneous Interlude 1920-2

I

The fates proved kinder to the blundering soloist than he deserved. Two years after my spectacular *debacle* at Hull, another by-election at Hastings landed me in the House of Commons with a safe seat in my pocket; in another two years I found myself on the Front Bench as a Parliamentary Secretary; and eighteen months after that I became a Cabinet Minister at the age of thirty-seven. Unfortunately, even this short apprenticeship was too long for my patience. This is not a personal chronicle, but the story of my restiveness may serve as a cautionary tale for future enthusiasts on the threshold of politics.

I had to earn my living and I was lucky enough to be offered a post in the Shell-Royal Dutch group of companies, in charge of the Anglo-Egyptian oilfields. But I was too intent on politics to make much of that opportunity. For instance, I had already become a member of the L.C.C. and Vice-Chairman of their Housing Committee; and in 1920 I allowed myself to become responsible for managing their Housing Bond campaign. It was a symptom of the amateurishness of social reform administration in those days that I should have spent the best part of a year in raising by popular subscription a mere £3,000,000 or so, which might have been raised more easily and more cheaply by an ordinary public loan. The campaign had its uses in the mobilization of public opinion and in making the metropolitan boroughs more conscious of the unity of the County of London; but it is sad to think that most of the money was sunk in that most amateurish of enterprises for which I must also share the responsibility: the building at Becontree of a new dormitory township without social centres or any other equipment for the development of a community life. For the rest, I suppose the campaign earned me some reputation for "drive", but that sort of reputation is of doubtful value in English politics; I should have done better in my own interest to have spent my time in making a little money or a more sober reputation in business. Probably no man should enter Parliament in order to satisfy an ambition for executive office; membership of the House of Commons should be accepted as a satisfying employment in itself. But, at any rate, the man with executive ambitions should have his own independent niche in the community, in business or in a profession, to which he can retreat when the lottery of power goes against him. If the "muckrakers" would only believe it, the public interest is less endangered by the private interests of Ministers than by their dependence upon the public favour. This choice between bias and rootlessness is the dilemma of government-making in a parliamentary democracy of the English type, especially in days when economic trends and State policy have combined to destroy the older independence of inherited wealth; and this dilemma has been hardly touched by giving salaries to back-bench Members of Parliament.

My other mistake in these years, after I entered the House of Commons in 1921, was to try to make a premature impression on the House by a rather feverish criticism of the Coalition Government. In that I was honest enough, for Lloyd George's agilities, both in home and foreign policy, seemed to me, more and more, to be grossly out of harmony with the primary need of both Britain and Europe for a settlement of minds and a concentration of purpose. But my criticism was often petulant and sometimes unjust; and one or two of my attacks upon Lord Curzon's handling of foreign relations, in particular, were resented by their target with an intensity which I did not expect. I was told later that, at the end of 1922 when Bonar Law was forming his government, Curzon had summarily dismissed the Prime Minister's suggestion that I might become his Parliamentary Under-Secretary at the Foreign Office. On the whole, I did not at the time much regret that missed opportunity, for I had had no experience of European diplomacy and had resigned from the Foreign Service partly because I distrusted my fitness for it, after my free and easy years in the United States. If I feel any regret now, it is only because the post might have enabled me to play some small part in my old, and then sadly neglected, field of Anglo-American relations.

2

Curzon was one of the few impressive figures on the political scene of 1921–2 who "dated" obviously from an earlier era – and the only one, I think, who was quite unconscious of the fact. It is curious to think how few these figures were. Balfour would have been unique in any period, and seemed, if anything, more at home as the elder statesman of the post-war world than he had been ten years before as the discarded leader of the Conservative party. It is given to few public men, between the ages of sixty-nine and eighty, to initiate, for good or ill, two such novel policies as the Jewish national home in Palestine and the Washington treaty of naval disarmament. Churchill, too, had never been typical of an era, and he was still a young man, as youth is reckoned in politics, and younger in nature than in years; he was in fact the only member of the government who, in this parliament, was adding visibly to his reputation by his handling of the Middle East and of Ireland. Lloyd George, it seemed to me, was engaged in wasting an enormous renown; but it was the renown of a war Minister which had blotted out his earlier controversial character as a social reformer and an unorthodox Chancellor of the Exchequer. The only "dating" figures seemed to be three: Curzon, Asquith and Austen Chamberlain.

I need not linger over any sketch of Curzon, for his portrait has been painted often enough by others. But I knew him just well enough to protest against the description of him as a "legendary cold fish" which I happened to see in a press review while writing this chapter. Dated as he was, he was never a Mr. Darcy. He was always a little larger than life-size, both in public and in private life, and, if he failed to fit comfortably into either after his return from India, his stature was the chief cause of his failure. A subsidiary cause, I suspect, was connected with a general misconception about the old "governing class". In another recent press review, I saw Palmerston quoted as an example of a virtue "rare in aristocrats": a capacity, and even a liking, for the drudgery of detailed work. On the contrary, I think that taste was one of the distinguishing marks of the public men of the Old Order, who cared much for the form and language of State Papers – and, for that matter, of private correspondence – and were not brought up to work with stenographers. Curzon certainly had this taste for clerical labour and lavished it on a hundred activites, archaeological, academic and domestic, besides his political work. No man could keep his mind fresh under the strain of such routine, combined with the burden of constant pain and infirmity. In modern days he would have killed three secretaries under him; as it was, he could only kill himself.

Asquith too, belonged unmistakably to the Old Order; but he had ceased, by that time, to convey its atmosphere. He seemed to have lapsed into a habit of almost consciously caricaturing his old parliamentary manner – rather ludicrously so sometimes, as when, in a rare moment of would-be solemnity, he once misquoted: "if these things be done in the dry bone, what shall be done in the green". He was, of course, in his decline; but it had never, within my memory, been easy to reconcile his apparently slipshod handling of great issues with the universal admiration felt for him by civil servants and soldiers who had known him as a departmental chief. I think he must have been always one of those men who think through administration to policy and whose instinct for policy becomes unsure when direct administrative responsibility ceases and its memories grow stale. Haldane was probably another instance, although he retained until his death an astonishing, and sometimes exasperating, appetite for novelty, whereas Asquith tended increasingly to live in the past.

In an utterly different way, the most representative and the most attractive of these "dating" figures was Austen Chamberlain. In 1921–2 he was in no sense played out; not yet sixty, the climax of his career was still before him. But he was already almost alone in his sense of parliamentary *style*. If that style inclined a little to the pompous, so much the better; the House of Commons was too august for mere business statements; it deserved to be treated in the grand manner. And this grand manner was not just a matter of form; it was the expression of a very conscious and articulate feeling for the essential virtues of British public life. I cannot do better than repeat here what I wrote of him twenty years ago, in an obituary notice; though it is based on fuller knowledge of him than I had in the earlier days of which I am now writing.

"Public duty can never be the same as private; where that dualism is not recognized, there can be neither freedom nor justice. But, while more logical peoples have accepted it as a principle to be defined, Englishmen have regarded it rather as an evil to be minimized. To us *raison d'etat*, like temptation, is a platitude which no responsible person will plead in defence of his actions. We cling to the belief that the dualism which cannot be reconciled in thought can and must be reconciled in life. The sort of integrity we demand of our statesmen and our administrators is an integration of private with public honour.

Austen Chamberlain was, above all, the embodiment of that integrity. He once said that his only conception of diplomatic negotiation was to lay his cards on the table. That is almost a description of his career, the explanation of his honourable successes and of his still more honourable failures. In public and in private life his cards were always on the table, and he would play only with the one pack. His most obvious cards, the trumps he seemed most often to declare, were perhaps the old-fashioned ones of the gentleman's code; loyalty to his Prime Minister, insistence on resignation under public censure, mediation by straight dealing. He played these with the old sense of good form in action, with the old grand manner in public speech. But these alone did not represent the real strength of his hand. He was acutely sensitive to the characteristic moralities and

[1] In *Public Administration*, March 1937.

charities of Englishmen. He was a social reformer, not only on public principle, but by private sentiment. And he was not afraid of being sentimental. Few men who have jumped young into the highest office have had the same feeling for the "social services" as he. Especially, perhaps, he had an understanding passion for education. The word is not too strong; his own ideal of conservatism was a "passionate moderation". He loved to show that quality in talk with young men and to arouse it in them. In his most difficult days, when the young men of his own party were in half-revolt against his leadership, no one could discuss their grievances more sympathetically in private or offer them more tolerant advice.

It was this mind in him, fortified by long experience, that gave him his acknowledged grasp of British parliamentary government. Others have known its rules and conventions as well as he; but none in our day has so entered into its spirit. He did not approve it detachedly; it was his natural climate; he lived and rejoiced in it. The climate was determined by certain factors which must be preserved at all costs; but, given these, it was a temperate climate affording the fullest scope to activity and innovation. Of these factors, the two crucial ones were the relation of Member to elector and of Minister to civil servant. In these two were focused all the problems of legislature and executive, of the respective functions of Crown, Cabinet and Parliament. Characteristically, he thought of both as personal relationships. Without some real personal touch with individuals, a Member of Parliament could not honestly claim to represent his constituents; where, as in India, such touch was impossible, honesty (the private virtue transmuted into public policy) must acknowledge the need for indirect election. Again, without intimate give and take between Minister and permanent official, neither could discharge his proper responsibility: the Minister for what to do, the civil servant for how to do it. That distinction was, in the last resort, clear; upon its maintenance rested the whole structure of government; but it must allow for every gradation of advice and argument before the final issue was reached. More personally still, the two were guardians of each other's honour; the Minister must make promises which the official must fulfil; the official, publicly criticized, must be defended by the Minister's admission of responsibility and purged, in the last resort, by the Minister's resignation.

Of course, these are commonplaces, but they are commonplaces only in England, and there only by grace of men like Chamberlain who are not ashamed to live by them. In these days when it is our fashion, both in government and in business administration, to talk much about technique, there is more than a little danger that they may be forgotten. Chamberlain commanded all the old technique of politics; he was interested in all the new. But he put technique in its right, its subordinate, place. Efficiency is the easiest of the public virtues; human sincerity the most difficult. Representativeness and responsibility are the two fundamental understandings upon which the British people are governed. They are our *flammantia moenia mundi*. Are they realities; can the Member of Parliament speak for the people; does the Minister mean what he says when he tells Parliament: 'this was done by my orders'? It was upon these tests that Chamberlain insisted; and it was because, throughout his public life, he had consistently measured his own conduct by them, that he was acknowledged, at his life's end, in the real though not in the formal sense, as the father of the House of Commons."

3

It was tragic to watch, in 1921–2, Chamberlain's integrity carrying him into an impossible parliamentary position. But before I say anything about the breakdown of the Coalition experiment in those years, I must glance at another aspect of my all too schizophrenic life at the time.

Though I wasted my opportunities in the Shell group, I took my work in Egypt seriously enough. It was by no means a full-time job, but it involved periodical visits to Cairo and the oil fields on the Red Sea coast, with side excursions to Khartoum and

F

Jerusalem, and it gave me at least a glimpse of how Englishmen were handling their overseas responsibilities after the interruption of the war. The impression I got was a curious one.

In one of his stories, Rudyard Kipling has described the typical bungalow of a junior official in the India of the 1880s, with its makeshift furnishing: "it was as though everything had been unpacked the night before to be repacked next morning". This recalls uncomfortably the description, written a few years later, of the typical house of a Turkish official in Europe: "The very aspect of a Turkish house seems to indicate that it is not intended as a permanent residence. . . . The general impression left on a European is that a party of travellers have occupied an old barn and said, 'let us make the place clean enough to live in. . . . We shall probably be off again in a week'."[1] Far-fetched as that comparison may seem, it is a useful reminder that no country can, in the long run, be governed by foreigners who cannot make it their home and would not if they could, even though they unselfishly sacrifice their whole working life to its welfare. Mere administration, however beneficent, strikes no permanent roots. If the foreigner is to perpetuate his rule, or even his influence, he must make, or promote, some more permanent investment in what, for him, is only the land of his temporary exile – whether it takes the form of schools and colleges or medical clinics, or the form of capital invested in productive enterprises.

The American diplomatist, Mr. William Phillips, in his reminiscences of his special mission to India in 1942–3, mentions among the legitimate anxieties of Britain in India the protection of her large "vested interests' there. This is a typical American misconception, for, in fact, the distinguishing mark of British "imperialism", ever since the passing of the East India Company, had been a rooted distrust of all vested interests. Trade, yes; but preferably conducted at arm's length; the fewer Englishmen who were tempted to settle down among "backward peoples" to create race and labour problems or unwittingly offend susceptibilities, the better. Even when, at the end of the nineteenth

[1]"Odysseus" (Sir Charles Eliot) *Turkey in Europe* 1900.

century, Joseph Chamberlain was at the Colonial Office, Mary Kingsley was almost alone in feeling: "In my attempt to tackle the government of native races in West Africa, all the holding ground I can find is along the commercial anchorage." At the end of the war, I had been shocked by Walter Long's hostility at the Colonial Office to American capital investment in Malaya; and later, in the 1930s, when I was involved in the Indian constitutional problem, I was even more struck by the complaint of a Hindu University professor, after his first shop-gazing tour of London. Why, he asked me, had India, the land of sweetmeat-eaters, where bazaar sweetmeats are an ever present danger to child life, never been given the chance of learning from England the art of modern confectionery? That instance is trivial and may be contentious: but it suggests the truth that the chief vice of "imperialism" of the English type may be the very reverse of exploitation; it may, on the contrary, be the diffidence which sets so high a price on orderly administration that it discourages racial contacts, lest they generate disturbing frictions or even change settled habits.

It may seem a far cry from Malaya, India or West Africa to Egypt; but the main difference lay, after all, in the special ambiguity of the position of the British official in Egypt as ostensibly an adviser, not a direct administrator; and this ambiguity only accentuated his nervousness about foreign contacts. And my first sight of Cairo at Christmas 1919 made me wonder whether, Englishmen being what they were, this nervousness might not, after all, have been justified. Certainly the foreign contacts which had been forced on Egypt since 1914, when she had become a base of military operations, had done much to spoil the whole atmosphere of relations between Egyptians and their English-speaking guardians. It was not a question of the riotous behaviour of some rougher elements in the armies of the Empire; it was, rather, a new tendency to think of Egyptians in terms of an army slang expressing the humorous contempt of decent young English fighting men for an unwarlike population. Former officials, returning after war service elsewhere, were shocked to hear this new language which lumped together the fellaheen of the Delta and the mixed populations of Cairo and Alexandria under the generic name of "Gippo". This, together with worse tales from war-time India, brought home to me that, in this field of Britain's overseas responsibilities, the old talk, of a "governing class" had been only too true, though in a very special sense. We had bred from selected university graduates and army officers of the old school a little corps of overseas civil servants, engineers and police-men to whom Santayana's famous phrase about "sweet, just, boyish masters" might perhaps fairly be applied; but this picked band was still pitifully unrepresentative of their fellow-country-men as a whole, or even of the social class to which they themselves belonged. It may have been the tragedy of the Empire between the wars that the statesmen of the later nineteenth century had made an imperial policy, but had neglected to make, in any serious sense, an imperially minded nation. For after all, if imperial-mindedness be at all a matter of educated manners, we had not begun to have a national system of secondary education until a bare twelve years before the outbreak of war.

Yet, making all due allowance for nervousness born of recent disturbing experiences, it is difficult to describe the sheer dis-comfort of discussing with Anglo-Egyptian officials the affairs of an infant Egyptian industry managed by Englishmen and Dutch-men. I do not want to make heavy weather of these discomforts, relieved as they were by much personal kindness; they were, in any case, temporary and faded rapidly enough on better acquaint-ance. Suffice it to say that, at first, so far as any Englishmen can be so silly, the frame of mind of these officials was like that of Dr. Moussadeq in Persia thirty years later. They utterly misconceived the character and policy of the business men with whom they had to deal. Of course, all "concessionaires" are potentially danger-ous animals, and these animals had acquired a peculiarly bad name in the shark-infested waters of Egyptian government; but the dangers of this particular concession were not at all the dangers apprehended by the office-holders at Cairo. It was, I think, signifi-cant that I met no such difficulties in the Sudan, though it is true that my business there was much less important or contentious. There I had a glimpse of a young and self-reliant administration, unhampered by old habits of exclusiveness or by any present ambiguities in their position. The contrast seemed to me to be symbolized by the first young recruits of the Sudan Plantations Syndicate with whom I travelled south from Cairo in that New Year of 1920.

These were, I think, my first crude impressions; I do not know how soon I came to realize that the real weakness of Anglo-Egyptian government was that it was already, even before the Declaration of 1922, a government in retreat. The only department of it that seemed securely in the saddle was represented by Russell Pasha, the commandant of the police, whose strength lay in no extraordinary abilities or personality, but in the simple fact that his heart was wholly in his job. How to conduct such retreats from the responsibilities of government was to be the main problem of British "colonial" policy for the next forty years; it is still our main problem today. It was, after all, not a new problem; in the very different field of the Dominions, colonized by European settlement, Britain had been working out its solution ever since Canada had begun to acquire responsible government more than half a century earlier. How to apply this experience to the progressive relinquishment of autocratic responsibilities in the colonies and in India was to be the headache of British statesmanship between the wars; it is still its headache today. But in Egypt, already in 1919, the coming retreat had a special quality of drift, for there it was a withdrawal from no fixed position, certainly from no autocratic one. We had restored Egypt's financial solvency; we had immensely improved the drainage and irrigation of her soil; we had reformed her police; we had taken an interest in her schools, just in so far as was necessary to produce a supply of government clerks; but, beyond that, we were relinquishing no clearly defined responsibilities, no solid cultural influence, and no large programme of social reform or economic development. We were advisers, and on the whole trusted advisers, of a genuinely Egyptian government, but that government was in the hands of

perhaps the worst governing class that has ever cursed a country –
for the most part, a landed class whose existence blocked the one
great social reform that the country required. I do not know how
history will judge the Declaration of 1922. I supported it in
principle at the time; but at once the best defence and the most
damning criticism of it is that the points it reserved to the discretion of the British Government nearly covered the only responsibilities which we had in fact been discharging in the three years
which proceeded it; the protection of Egypt against foreigners
and the protection of foreigners in Egypt; the Sudan; and the
security of the communications of the British Empire. Except for
the Sudan, these responsibilities were almost reducible to the
maintenance of a military occupation and deserved the criticism
contained in an old aphorism of Bismarck: "You can do a great
deal with bayonets; but you cannot sit upon them." But to all
this I shall have to return later in my story.

4

The Parliament of 1919–22 will be remembered in history
chiefly for the manner of its end. My own tiny part in that end
was as the youngest member of the youngish group of back-bench
Conservatives whom the insurgent die-hard wing of the party had
dubbed "the mugwumps".

Some historians will judge, as some critics judge now, that the
revolt of the Tory party at the Carlton Club meeting, was a
disastrous mistake, because it destroyed the chance of a true fusion
between the Tory and Liberal parties. Such a fusion, under the
heat generated by Lloyd George's energy and resourcefulness,
would, they say and will say, have produced a healthier alternative party to Labour than the personal ascendancy which Baldwin
was to win over a great body of non-partisan Liberal opinion in
the constituencies. It would not have left a rump Liberal party
struggling to regain a foothold in the House of Commons, but
would have prepared a fold wide enough to receive the whole
party on Asquith's death. As so often happens, they will conclude,

the price which the country had to pay for Tory independence did
not fall due until ten years later, when a Lloyd George-Chamber-
lain-Churchill Coalition might have saved it from a period of
disastrously negative government under the twin leadership of
Macdonald and Baldwin.

As might-have-beens go, that would be quite a reasonable case
for the prosecution; though my own estimate of might-have-
beens is different. Undoubtedly the country had to pay a price for
Tory independence, but the main price had to be paid immediately, in the following two years. I shall have more to say about
this later. But before any such might-have-beens are made the
basis for a verdict against the Carlton Club meeting, several other
considerations would have to be taken into account. One would
be the curious flavour of disreputability which haunted the Lloyd
George administration. For all I actually know, the flavour may
have been largely imagined, but it certainly offended many not
over-sensitive palates, and by those whom it offended it was
universally ascribed to Lloyd George's personal cookery. I do not
think it was mainly attributable to the "honours" scandals which
eventually brought him to book in a well-known debate in the
House of Commons; its most significant symptom seemed, rather,
to be that the Civil Service did not feel safe with him. The integrity of the Service, it was said, had been barely protected
against his encroachments at the end of the war by the toughness
of the Civil Service Commission and especially of its Chairman,
Sir Stanley Leathes. It was, I think, out of that fight that there
emerged the novel figure of a Head of the Civil Service, in the
person of the Permanent Secretary of the Treasury; whose
function it was to ensure that Prime Minister's appointments in
government departments should be made on non-political advice.
That experiment was to prove how dangerous it is to crystallize
the basic conventions of the British constitution into formal
institutions and how dangerous, therefore, it was to allow those
conventions to be interpreted by a Prime Minister who had no
instinctive feeling for them – who could be described, as one of
his war-time colleagues once described him to me, in somewhat

Darcyish terms, as "a very able little man, and in some ways a very wise little man, but he doesn't know how to behave".

Nor, of course, was the civil servant's sense of insecurity due solely to this apprehension of temperamental jobberies; it was due much more, probably, to the abrupt reversals of policy which had disfigured the last two years of the Coalition: in Ireland, in Turkey, in housing, in education, in the whole atmosphere created by the Geddes Committee. Five years later Lord Lloyd was to write from Cairo, in a very different connection: "Believing as I do that clarity is the essence of statesmanship and that solutions based upon a series of hopeless ambiguities only aggravate the mischief."[1] Those words express well enough the feelings not only of the senior civil servant, a life-long Liberal, who told me, after the election of 1922, that he had voted Conservative for the first time in his life, solely in order to keep Lloyd George out of power, but also of all those elements in the Tory party with whom I had found myself most in sympathy since I entered Parliament.

But how much is a Tory party worth in the political life of a country like Btitain? That is the other main consideration which the future historian will have to take into account. Perhaps I am not a good judge of that question; I have never been much of a party man; coalitions suit me well enough, though my bump of argumentativeness in debate has usually prevented me from carrying conviction as a candidate for office in coalition governments. But my acquaintance with American and Canadian politics led me early to believe that there can be no intelligent radicalism in a country where there is no intelligible conservative tradition. Eccentricity, if it is to be a rational adventure and not mere restlessness, must be a conscious departure from a recognized norm and, if it is not to be mere revolt, the norm must be something more than a defence of things as they are. Such a norm must be embodied in a political organization, a party. But, in 1922, the existence of such a party in Britain had been in danger for nearly twenty years. An Oxford contemporary who had entered politics before the war used to tell me then that the Conservative party

[1] Forbes Adam, *Life of Lord Lloyd.*

had lost its moral authority in the country ever since it had treated its victory in the "Khaki" election of 1900 as a mandate for a long term of peace-time government. There was just enough truth in that judgment to put the younger Tories on their guard against misusing the mandate given them in a moment of still more heedless enthusiasm at the end of a greater war. There was, indeed, in the autumn of 1922, no question of stretching the mandate of 1918 to cover a longer term of office, for all were agreed on the necessity of an early General Election. But there was very much a question of asking the electors for a renewed vote of confidence in the leadership of one man whom most Tories had in fact come to distrust profoundly; and that, one felt, was not the way to restore the damaged moral authority of their party.

The Coalition was, in fact, too much Lloyd George's personal following, and it stood or fell with his personal reputation. The only way to preserve it would have been the one proposed by Lloyd George himself earlier that year, when he offered to retire or to serve under Chamberlain as Prime Minister. I felt at the time that Chamberlain's refusal of this offer was as misguided as it was honourable. Now I am not so sure; Chamberlain's apparently useless self-sacrifice may have been part of the price that the Tory party had to pay for its moral restoration. And, as usual, the price was paid by the innocent.

The historical importance of these considerations lies mainly in the influence they exerted then and later on the mind of one man: Stanley Baldwin. In all the sketches that have been made of his character since his death, this point has, I think, been too often missed. More than once, in later days, he told me how he had sat in that Cabinet as a "new boy", saying little, but watching what went on, and wondering whether the government of England "would ever be clean again". I will not embroider these bare words by speculating how an atmosphere which Baldwin found so morally repugnant could have been tolerable to others, and especially to Chamberlain with his strong sense of constitutional proprieties. There are several possible explanations honourable to both men. But my point here is, not that Baldwin's moral judgment was necessarily sound, but that it affected his whole subsequent attitude to political problems. His pre-occupation, emphasized by commentators like G. M. Young, with the education of the Labour party as the source of the alternative governments of the future, arose from a sense, not merely of the Labour party's rawness, but rather of the moral risks run by all parties in the transition between an old order and a new. In that connection, his mind played constantly round the half-myth of the "lost generation"—the idea that the gradual supersession of age by youth, the natural way in which a tradition is preserved and transmitted, had been almost fatally interrupted by the casualties of the war.

Indeed, I think that the chief criticism that might be made of Baldwin's record is that he tended to measure all problems of policy by their relation to the integrity of the party which he led. His instinctive use of that measuring rod often startled, and sometimes shocked, me. It was natural enough that he should produce such a yardstick at the Carlton Club meeting, and that, in his running fight with Rothermere and Beaverbrook, he should think of himself chiefly as saving the soul of his party. I once repeated to him my friend's idea of the party's loss of moral authority in the first decade of the century; and he commented that perhaps it was some such feeling that had prompted him to the escapade of the general election of 1923. I found this easy to believe at the time, and I still think it easier to believe than the alternative theory that he was mainly influenced, on that occasion, by the fear that Lloyd George might be about to steal the protectionists' clothes. But when later, in discussing the Indian constitutional problem, he expressed to me his determination not to allow the Conservative party to be split over India as the old Liberal party had been split over Ireland, I confess that, though I agreed with his Indian policy, I almost gasped at the apparent inadequacy of its motive. This care for a party seemed to me then to be a relic of the past and it reminded me uncomfortably of the fervours of American party conventions at which I had learnt to laugh. Now, I am not so sure. The parties, as they had begun to emerge in both Britain and America about the fifties and sixties of the nineteenth century, were no longer the shifting factions of earlier days, and the oft-quoted tag about public men who "to party give up what was meant for mankind" is no longer a valid criticism of any public man, except the original philosopher or the rare political genius. Baldwin would certainly never have claimed to be either. Today, the newest school of academic political scientists are wont to begin their dissertations on parliamentary constitutions with a study of the organization of parties; and they may be right. Each party is, in a real sense, the trustee of national unity – more so than even parliament itself, which must move in an atmosphere of constant debate. If parties forget their trusteeship they make way all too easily for the single party of a national dictatorship. If the "party caucus" is still rightly a term of abuse, the judgments formed by a body of men and women who are accustomed to look at the problems of government from a certain point of view may be nevertheless, at most times, a better guide to policy than the flights of imagination which it is fashionable to describe by the cant name of "vision". And there may be such a thing as "vision" in party management. The man who allows a body of political opinion to degenerate into the familiar partisan brew of cold doctrine and hot prejudice, and is then content to live on it, has no place among statesmen; but there is a place in that company for the man who devotes himself to form and foster a body of political thought and morals, which, having the habit of unity, may outlast himself and even his memory, and may become, on occasion, the rallying point of a nation.

That is not my complete portrait of Baldwin; it must be read with much else that I shall have to say later.

CHAPTER VI

Educational Policies and Problems 1924-9

I

I will skip, for the moment, the story of the two Parliaments elected in the autumns of 1922 and 1923. What I have to say about those two years will be best said later, when I come to review the whole course of the first half of the "Twenty Years' Truce" from what seems to me the watershed of the General Election of 1929. I will pass, in the next two chapters, direct to my near-five years of office as President of the Board of Education in the second Baldwin administration.

Because this proved to be my introduction to what has become, in one form or another, my main work in life, I shall, no doubt, exaggerate its importance in what I write about it. But, making allowance for this prejudice, I think my term of office did at least mark the point at which all sections of English political opinion came to learn the lesson of the political importance of educational administration. It was a lesson for which most of them were ill-prepared. In my first days at the Board, a well-known octogenarian "character" of the time, a retired public school master and classical scholar of the old breed, but one who had interested himself actively in the work of his County Education Committee, said to me: "My dear boy, I am *very* glad to see you in this position. I once played bridge with a President of the Board, an ex-President and a Parliamentary Secretary. None of them knew anything about education; and one of them could not even play bridge." I should certainly have disappointed the old gentleman if he had ever tested me in either of these branches of culture; but the quip has stuck in my memory as a sort of verbal caricature of the normal place of education in political life during the forty-seven years between W. E. Forster and H. A. L. Fisher. New legislation might bring up a substantial personage like Forster, though, even so, it was notable that the Act of 1902 had to be personally handled by the Prime Minister; but administration was assumed to be the business of the permanent officials, on whom the politician President could be expected, at most, to keep a wary eye lest they offend the susceptibilities of sectarian supporters of the government, Anglican, Roman Catholic, Free Church or secularist. Apart from these susceptibilities, the building up of an effective national system of education by positive administration had never been regarded as a major political interest. Perhaps the one exception to this negligence was Acland in the government of 1892-5, for he at least had launched a much needed campaign against insanitary school buildings – of which more anon.

Lloyd George broke this tradition of carelessness with the appointment of Fisher; but, alas, he also started the new tradition of treating the field of education, which he had so recently under-taken to develop, as, for that very reason, the field also where economies in public expenditure could most easily be effected when the public purse-strings had to be tightened. To that he was, no doubt tempted by Fisher's miscalculations. Fisher had launched an ambitious programme of expansion, the cost of which he estimated at first at a mere £3,000,000; but in this estimate he had made no allowance for the inevitable improvement of teachers' salaries and pensions. The veteran secretary of the National Union of Teachers, Sir James Yoxall, had foreseen the consequent collapse and had not joined in the enthusiasm of his professional colleagues for Fisher's Education Bill, which he thought was an attempt to do too much in too many directions simultaneously. The increase in teachers' salaries flooded out most of Fisher's planned developments; and his last two years in office was a dis-couraging period of disappointed hopes. That was his legacy to his successor in 1922. A quarter of a century later Mr. Aneurin Bevan was to make a miscalculation of almost precisely the same kind in creating a too sudden socialized National Health service. It is, indeed, odd that statesmen never learn from the past and what they learn most slowly seems to be arithmetic.

In the first Macdonald administration of 1924, Charles Trevelyan found himself as much entangled in the wreckage of Fisher's plans as Edward Wood had been, and he got no more encouragement from Snowden at the Treasury than Wood had got from Baldwin or Chamberlain. But, having served a six-years' apprenticeship as Parliamentary Secretary of the Board before the war, he had the idea, the best available in the circumstances, of reviving, in effect, Acland's thirty-year-old campaign for the renovation or replacement of "black-listed" elementary schools, supplemented by a reduction in the numbers of over-large classes and a steady expansion of secondary education; and he made this the basis for what he suggested might be a ten-year programme of "continuity" to be followed by future governments of whatever party. I adopted that programme, which I felt would at any rate be useful housemaid's work beyond the criticism of even the most ardent economists living on memories of pre-war educational politics.

But, meanwhile, something was happening in the country which had hardly yet penetrated to the mind of any politician in Whitehall or Westminster. The demand for real "equality of opportunity" in education was becoming nothing less than the main popular motive for political action. In many minds, this demand was, no doubt, a very crude form of idolatry, or, at any rate, a gross exaggeration of the advantages which the old "governing classes" could be imagined to have derived from mere schooling. At its worst, it could become a rather repulsive design to use the State schools as instruments for propagating a revolutionary philosophy, as the "public" schools were supposed to have inculcated a philosophy of oligarchy. But in the mind of the average elector, the demand proceeded from a much simpler appetite for the best available standards of excellence in thought and manners and a not ignoble desire for access to the means of attaining such standards. And if those means were often conceived also as the means to power in the State for a new popular governing class, that did not necessarily render the desire less admirable. It was at least more admirable than some of the lazier motives which have prompted the more recent worship of a physical Welfare State. Its most dangerous tendency was to breed a rather sickly distaste for "vocational" education. That tendency had to be counteracted if any healthy form of national education was to emerge.

This distaste was bound up with a curious change in the popular meaning attached to the statutory phrase "elementary education" – a change which had hardly yet registered itself in the language of national policies. The phrase had ceased to mean a stage in education preparatory to higher studies for those who might be capable of them; it had come to mean a kind of education suitable to all who were to earn their living by manual labour. Elementary schools already retained their pupils for nearly three years after the age at which the cleverest of them had left to enter a grammar school; and those years were not deliberately designed as a preparation for anything, for there was as yet hardly any conscious relation between elementary and technical schools. At this stage, at any rate, elementary schools were, as such, no part of any "educational ladder"; they were as much "finishing" schools for manual workers as Miss Pinkerton's academy was a finishing school for young ladies; and a "class" education of this kind was coming to be increasingly suspected and resented.

In the middle twenties, this rising tide of feeling had hardly risen above the level of municipal politics, and national statesmen, even those with long experience of such politics, were quite unconscious of it. Not long after Baldwin formed his government, Neville Chamberlain said to me that, in his judgment, public opinion – at any rate, Conservative public opinion – would welcome more expenditure on health and housing, but was in favour of economies in education. This view was almost traditional in Birmingham. Fifty years before, Joseph Chamberlain, the Radical, had written, after a heated but disappointing educational campaign: "The Education question . . . has failed to evoke any great popular enthusiasm . . . the assistance of the working classes is not to be looked for without much extension of the argument." Unhappily his political heirs in his city had failed to notice how much the argument had in fact been extended in the course of half a century, though they were lucky enough to find in his nephew, Byng Kenrick, who was for many years Chairman of their Education Committee, one of the really great local educational administrators of the twentieth century. That discovery may have saved them from the revolution which swept their sister city of Sheffield in the autumn of 1926 when the Labour party won control of the City Council. Some years later, the leader in that "surprising judgment" said that he would guarantee to hold Sheffield for his party on the educational issue alone. The contrast between that statement and Neville Chamberlain's is significant.

In this respect, I am afraid I found the Chancellor of the Exchequer an even more archaic colleague than the Minister of Health. To tell the truth, Churchill's feelings about education have often reminded me, then and since, of Porson's famous comment on Gibbon's attitude to Christianity; he seemed to "hate it so cordially that he might seem to revenge some personal injury". In fact, of course, this was just the contempt felt by the really self-cultured genius for forms of boyhood schooling from which he himself felt he had derived no benefit. That contempt was, no doubt, accentuated by a generous disdain for the squalid sectarian controversies which had defaced educational policy during the first ten years of his political life, and he hardly realized how almost completely those squalors had evaporated since the war. Moreover, in all his varied experience, he had never administered a department which had to deal with local governments; and he was impatient of this kind of administration. His imagination would have been caught by the use of the taxpayer's money to build and staff some great national institution; but he could see no political or national advantage in the making of grants in aid of municipal institutions, from which the municipalities would reap most of the credit – whether it were the extension of the great Manchester College of Technology or the improvement of what he once described to me, in one of his baroque moments, as "village schools with a few half-naked children rolling in the dust". Churchill's country owes much to his baroque moods, but it is unfortunately not a style of architecture that suits educational building.

But, if I thus criticize two of my Conservative colleagues, their prejudices were shared by the older members of all parties. I think, for instance, that both Macdonald and Snowden shared with Churchill the impatience of the self-educated man with formal school education. All three were ready to encourage less formal schemes of adult education; but none of them had much sympathy with the reforming zeal of the younger men of their parties. It was much the same with the Liberal party. Asquith, to the day of his death, could see no point in the Act of 1902, and was unconscious of the renaissance of secondary education which it introduced. In this field, more than in most others, the war years had been a real dividing line between new and old schools of thought.

2

It fell to me to bring these old prejudices sharply up against the new current of public opinion. In the early spring of 1926, after a series of meetings with a Cabinet committee on economy, which brought me to the verge of resignation, I issued the notorious Circular 1371 to local education authorities, proposing a number of drastic checks on expansion. The storm of opposition which this aroused shocked my colleagues and even surprised myself. It was my first experience of a new sensitiveness in the enlarged post-war electorate. It had become fatally easy to arouse immoderate expectations by the use of even the most moderate language and equally immoderate resentment by even a temporary disappointment of those expectations.

Churchill was fond of recounting Haldane's skill in discrediting the advocates of Army retrenchment in 1906 by staging a ceremony at which King Edward bade a tearful farewell to a disbanded battalion of Scots Guards; and I have sometimes wondered whether he suspected me of a similar manoeuvre. For my circular was drowned in the flood of protests and my colleagues left me free thereafter to pursue my policy as best I could. But I could lay no claim to such political astuteness, even if I had thought it

G

honest. I was more influenced by a saying of Theodore Roosevelt that all unpleasant political fences should be taken at a gallop. On the whole I proved the advice to be sound on this occasion, though it was, I think, on this occasion that Neville Chamberlain first took a strong dislike to my style of horsemanship. Trevelyan warned me from the front Opposition bench that it could never be "glad confident morning again"; but it is the peculiarity of the educational hunting field that "glad confident morning" is altogether too exhilarating an atmosphere for a long run. In practice the system of percentage Exchequer grants allowed local authorities to incur, without effective Treasury control, liabilities which became at least as much Treasury liabilities as municipal. It is extraordinarily difficult, in such a riding school, for a Minister to strike the right balance between the use of the spur and bridle. My savage tug on the curb in 1926 was, no doubt, bad horsemanship, and it nearly landed me in the ditch; but it made it, perhaps, easier for me to strike something like the right balance over the next three years, and I think I can claim that, by the General Election of 1929, horse and rider had come to understand one another pretty well.

If I lost some political reputation by the incident, that was, on the whole, an advantage to my work. I had protested, I remember, to the Editor of the *Times* against the too frequent publication of my occasional addresses at school speech days and the like. They were the necessary local price I had to pay for getting personally to know schools and local authorities; but altogether too much was being made by the national press of what I thought of as "Percy's daily platitudes". After the flurry of 1926 I was glad to be able to get on with my work in the comparative obscurity to which political journalists tended to consign me for the next three years. To vary my metaphor, for the moment, from equitation to horticulture, schoolmasters will know what I mean when I say that education is a plant that thrives best in some shade, which may be why it is so seldom a favourite flower in any politician's garden.

It was the more important that local authorities and the Board should understand one another because I had added to the line of country marked out by Trevelyan a new line which involved the negotiation of some particularly difficult fences. I have never been sure of the origins of what came to be known as "Hadow re-organization": the splitting of elementary schools into two stages, junior and senior, with a "break" at about the age of eleven. I can only be sure that the policy did not originate with the Hadow report of 1926 on the *Education of the Adolescent*. My first memory of it is in a note on educational policy which I drew up for a group of Conservative Members of Parliament, for inclusion in the party's programme at the General Election of 1924. On the initiative of the Board's officials, it was propounded a few weeks later, as official policy in a circular (No. 1351) of January 1925. That I issued this circular without Cabinet, or even Treasury, sanction was characteristic, not so much of my own habits, as of the habits of educational administration in those days. The truth, I fancy, is that this policy had become a commonplace among educational administrators in England, as it had already long been in some continental countries, and that I took it up without quite realizing how far it would lead me. It was, in fact, to become the centre-piece of educational reform for the next thirty years. But it was far from being a commonplace among local authorities, especially those in rural areas, or among Anglicans or Roman Catholics who often viewed it as a threat to the entrenched position of Church schools; and it would never have "caught on" with public opinion but for the powerful advertisement given to the idea in the Hadow report. Even with that advertisement, the popularization of the idea became my main and most uphill task in office.

Here again, I felt I had to use the curb at an early stage in the hunt. The Hadow Committee had been logical, though again hardly original, in recommending the general raising of the compulsory school-leaving age from fourteen to fifteen, on the ground that otherwise the senior stage would not be long enough for what they conceived as a course of definitely secondary education. I thought this particular recommendation would divert the hunt too far from Trevelyan's and my chosen line of country and I publicly rejected it almost immediately after I received the report. This was probably unnecessary; it could have been allowed to remain, what it had long been in the teaching profession, a cherished aspiration the attainment of which must be postponed for severely practical reasons. I could have adduced overwhelming arguments for its postponement, as in fact I subsequently did; and those arguments would have carried more weight if I had not first seemed to challenge the aspiration itself.

This whole business is worth recording only because it was to turn out to be a glaring example of the difficulties of what has come to be known as "planning" in politics. The high birthrate of the years immediately after the war was creating a "bulge" in school population which would not begin to pass out of the elementary schools until about 1933–4. Re-organized schools planned for the school population of the late twenties would be large enough to take the extra age group in 1933–4; but to raise the school-leaving age before that date must either divert building unnecessarily from more urgent requirements or lead to a new over-crowding of classes and to all the evils of temporary make-shift accommodation. But though a raising of the age about 1933–4 was my tentative personal plan, I could not ask the Cabinet to adopt it as official policy in advance, because in 1926 or 1927 such a decision would have been a speculative mortgaging of future budgets for a project which could not be represented as popular with the general mass of the electorate. To be suspected of a desire to keep children longer at school was a black mark against parliamentary candidates in the constituencies in 1929 and later; and, in my experience, none were more eager to foment such suspicions than Labour canvassers. In fact, even in 1931, when Trevelyan attempted to enact the age of fifteen, his Bill foundered, partly on the issue of Church schools, but mainly from lack of real popular support. But by 1933–4 when the raising of the age would have been otherwise opportune, the Cabinet of the day was cowering under the impact of the economic blizzard, and, apart from the makeshift Act of 1936, the baby was passed on to Butler who had to adopt it in 1944 at the worst possible moment, on the eve of a new and more formidable "bulge" in school population. The resultant difficulties of school planning are with us as I write in 1956. Parliamentary government has many advantages; it can achieve reasonable continuity, but a sense of timing is never one of its virtues.

In another way, however, my mind did not move on quite the same lines as the Hadow report – or perhaps I should say, as the trend of public opinion which gathered round it and finally found expression in the Butler Act of 1944. It seemed to me unwise to lump together all schooling after the age of eleven under the name "secondary" and thus to stimulate the impossible demand for what is now termed "parity of esteem" between, for instance, the best grammar schools and such "county modern" schools as teach no language but English nor any chemistry or physics beyond the elements of the craft called "rural science". My thoughts ran rather on a different "parity of esteem" (and would that educational discussions were not so fertile in dog-English catch-words!) – a parity between two educational "ladders", one leading through the secondary school to the university, the other through the senior and technical schools to the college of technology, with ample facilities for changing from one to the other at almost any rung. In mountaineering, it is the summits that are of equal worth according to the climber's taste and purpose. No one can equate the lower or middle slopes of Skiddaw with the cliffs of the Cuillin; but "the red glare on Skiddaw" may summon more people to more effective national service than any beacon on the peaks of Skye. That is why I did my best to revive national interest in technical education, and to encourage more regional consultation in its development, though I cannot claim to have been what one writer has called me, with the partiality of an ex-private secretary, "the first President of the Board who really grasped the full implications of technical education".[1]

It was for this reason that I could never feel much enthusiasm for the raising of the school-leaving age. The cutting of education

[1] G. A. N. Lowndes, *The Silent Social Revolution*, O.U.P., 1937.

into convenient administrative lengths, and especially the de-
marcation of certain schools as catering for "compelled" pupils,
seemed to me subtly out of focus with the idea of stages of
learning wide open at their tops for climbers who desired to go
higher. This is perhaps no more than a difference of taste, but I
would rather have offered facilities and incentives to the growing
popular desire for higher education, than use the whip of compul-
sion over a fixed distance on horses many of whom were only too
willing to go much farther. This feeling led me into what was
perhaps an absurdity which puzzled my most benevolent colleagues, like Austen Chamberlain: my attempt, in the election of
1929, to substitute the phrase "higher education for all" for the
popular catchword "secondary education for all".

3

These memories of old debates may seem but the stirring of
dregs; but in truth they are a little more than that. After all, the
children passing through the schools of 1924–9 were to be the men
of the Battle of Britain, of the Desert Rats and the Normandy
beaches. They were, later, to be the technicians of a nation
struggling to pay its way in a world impoverished by war.
Schooling may not have much to do with the making of a soldier;
it was a very unschooled breed of Englishmen whom Sir John
Moore had trained, more than a century before, to be the finest
soldiers in Europe. But the training camps of 1940 had to deal with
very different material from the Shorncliffe of 1802; they had to
deal, not with the sharp senses and independent mind of a Dorset
shepherd like Rifleman Harris, or even of the "village bad hats"
who were often his comrades; they had to deal with minds dulled
and senses blunted by four generations of urban over-crowding
and two of agricultural depression. Schools may seldom be able
to create; perhaps their main task must always be no more than to
counteract the crude influences of contemporary life; but the
English schools that emerged from World War I were in some
ways dangerously unsuited to that task. In some ways; yet, if I
now set myself to criticize, let me testify at the outset that the

main impression that I carried away with me from these years was of the essential soundness of English school teachers.

What influences had they to counteract? First and foremost, a revolutionary frame of mind. I hope the historian of the future will not underrate the reality of that trend of English thought in the 'twenties, just because some contemporaries were needlessly scared by it. Lloyd George no doubt grossly over-dramatized the Coal Strike of 1921, when he recalled troops from the Continent and embodied the Territorial Army; in 1925, a wiser Home Office, preparing to meet the more serious threat of the coming General Strike, proceeded coolly on the calculation that, as one of its senior officials said to me in rejecting my fussy pleas for more drastic precautions, though Communists might play some part in fomenting the trouble, "there is not a barricade man among them". Yet, in everything except its violence, the Russian Revolution was admired in those days by very many Englishmen, and they showed perhaps a characteristic tendency to play verbally with the fire they did not mean to light. Such word-play is, from the educational point of view, the worst sin that men can commit; but in some quarters it was then regarded almost as a positive principle of education. Nowadays, when Englishmen – and not least socialist Englishmen – have acquired so deep a horror of "brain-washing" and the corruption of youth by propaganda, it seems hard to believe that, for instance, the Labour Conference at Margate in 1926 should have called for an investigation into "how far, under a workers' administration . . . a proletarian attitude and outlook on life might be cultivated" in the schools. But that resolution was in fact passed, and was, perhaps, not uninfluenced by the feeling expressed, a few months earlier, by a London docker to one of the Board's inspectors at the end of the General Strike: "We have lost this strike, because the public-school spirit has got into the elementary schools."

The inspector took that remark as an unintended compliment to twenty years of unpretentious and ill-paid school teaching, since the days when an earlier inspector had written: "Our elementary boy has hardly the most elementary idea of schoolboy honour. . . .

From this beginning he easily arrives at the deadly vice of the working class, the incapacity for playing fair and for playing without quarrelling."[1] There would have been some truth in such a compliment, even though the performances of "our elementary boy", from 1914 to 1918 and from Flanders to the Persian Gulf, had cast some doubt on the earlier judgment. But I confess that I was more inclined to take the remark as a warning. In those days of post-war shell-shock, English education stood in some danger of splitting, in spirit as well as in texture, into two rival "class" systems.

On the whole, since the revolution of 1902 the tendency had been the other way. The independent "public" schools had not held aloof from the new breed of council and grant-aided second-ary schools. The headmasters of the larger schools of the new breed (which were often old endowed grammar schools with a long and distinguished local history, but fallen on evil times before 1902) were already powerfully diluting the aristocracy of the Headmasters' Conference, and some of the older of these schools were beginning to teach an even wider social range of pupils than had come to them in the seventeenth and early eighteenth centuries before the "public" schools had started a new fashion of social segregation. And, anyway, that fashion had never degener-ated into an ideal; public school masters had, on the whole, been pretty consistently intent on counteracting the inclination of both Mr. Darcy's and Mr. Gardiner's great grandchildren towards social exclusiveness. But the generation of those families who had grown to school age during the war – often without a father's guidance – were, perhaps, proving less malleable. The trouble about an "upper class" is that its members can more easily learn generosity when their social position is unchallenged and their wealth secure than when they begin to find themselves obliged to accept heavy taxation and to meet the subsidized rivalry of their less priveleged countrymen. There was just enough of the *émigré* temper among the public school boys of that generation to make one fear lest the national unity of the future might be crushed out

[1] Sneyd-Kynnersley *H.M.I.* 1908.

between the competing resentments of artisans and gentry, both conscious of having made great sacrifices in the war, but both disappointed – the one of the promised "land fit for heroes to live in", and the other of their natural expectation of the opportunities enjoyed by their fathers.

These fears proved liars in England, though, be it remembered, not on the Continent of Europe, and it is well not to forget how far the proof in England was against all reasonable expectation in the middle 'twenties, nor how much it may have owed to English school teachers.

In another respect, however, English school-teachers were perhaps less successful. Educational philosophy had become dangerously romantic since the war, the more dangerously so because it was being encouraged by, for instance, the American school of Dewey to clothe its romance in the trappings of science and to dignify it by the title of psychology. This romantic science felt most at home in the nursery and infant schools. It aimed at civilizing children rather than at instructing them; and it assumed – *o sancta simplicitas* – that the social virtues need not be inculcated but would develop naturally if only the child could be brought to school young enough and protected to that extent from the crudities of his home environment. Its ideal was a nursery school place for every child from the age of two. Thenceforward, the good teacher must ensure the "happy unfolding" of the child's personality. At a later stage in my educational work I could not help sympathizing with the outburst of an old bachelor university professor after listening to this view being propounded by a candidate for a lectureship in the education of young children: "nonsense, nonsense; a child ought to be brought up to *expect unhappiness*". If that maxim sounds cruel, it must be remembered that the new romantic science had an ugly side of its own. Believing in free development it believed also that the individual's capacity for development was predetermined at birth and that its limits could be measured in advance. The individual's "intelligence quotient" could be ascertained at an early age, at any rate by the age of eleven; and it was unalterable. "He that developeth not naturally is damned already" came near to be the central doctrine of this new theology; for those who cannot believe in the daylight fact of original sin fall easy victims to the calvinistic nightmare of predestination.

Of course, these were the theories of "educationalists" who were seldom in daily contact with children; and school teachers were generally immunized by experience against their worst exaggerations. But they tended nevertheless to give a sort of infantile bias to all "elementary" education. In the reaction against cramming, the idea of a "general education" was coming to mean little more than an infantile process of "taking notice"; the child's fundamental appetite for new *knowledge* was not satisfied and his later competitive ambition to *excel* in knowledge was discouraged. Perhaps the modern tendency to over-specialization in secondary schools is due, more often than its critics realize, to the reaction of fifth – and sixth – form pupils themselves against the shallow wateriness of the "general education" in which they have splashed for their first ten years in school without being given the chance of going anywhere along the beach where the water is deep enough for swimming.

No doubt much of this was no more than the normal periodic swing of the pendulum between two quite valid conceptions of education: the cultivation of manners and the discipline of the intellect. But in those years the swing was accentuated by something unpleasantly like a flight from reality. War had become an unthinkable horror; the earlier reaction against mere "drum and trumpet" history, for instance, had been heightened by the nightmare of four years of trench warfare. That obsession will have to be reckoned with by the future social historian and in the 'twenties it operated nowhere more dangerously than on the teaching profession. This, after all, was the truth about war, not the *panache* of Agincourt or Ramillies or Salamanca; and the thoughts of children must be deliberately directed away from that horror to the serenities of the League of Nations. Better still, let their thoughts be kept at home; let them begin to learn history from their village, from the old brasses of the parish church or from the traces of open field and common and enclosure in the country-side; but let the crusaders' tombs in the church remain to them no more than a barbaric fairy tale and let them never remember how their more modern forebears had left this quiet home to march with Marlborough to the Danube or, it may be, to cross the Rockies with Brigham Young.

This tendency, in the manner of the Duke in *As You Like It*, to translate the stubbornness of human fortune into as quiet and sweet a style as possible was, perhaps, accentuated by a fashion in Biblical criticism which was already becoming out of date among scholars, but (as so often happens) had just begun to affect Scripture teaching in the schools. To speak only of the more secular aspects of that fashion, its outstanding feature seemed to me to be its lack of historical sense. The critics, trained mainly in the ancient languages and in philosophy, had been so busy reducing the Jehovah of the Pentateuch to the stature of a tribal deity with more than doubtful morals, that they hardly allowed their disciples to catch a glimpse of the agonies through which human societies have, in fact, had to struggle towards civilization, or of the price in blood and tears which the most favoured among them have had to pay for their rare moments of enlightenment and peace. In a world where Victorian hopes of natural progress had already been so terribly disappointed, we were still trifling with the soothing syrups of Edwardian days; we were still trying to teach history without its cataclysms and religion without its responsibilities of belief and worship. And this was the world which was so soon to learn that old tales were true after all, and to renew its ancient experience of tyrants and captivities, of idolatries and martyrdoms.

Of course these childishnesses (if teachers will forgive me the word) fitted well enough into the setting of purely "elementary" education; in that setting they were, indeed, a shining contrast to the contemporary craze, in some continental countries, for raising the moral temperature of school children by appeals to their emotions; and, in that setting, there was, perhaps, little in them to alarm even the most old-fashioned administrator in Whitehall who, anyway, was mercifully precluded by sound tradition from any attempt to dictate modes of teaching in the schools. After all, the aim of early education must always be, in some degree, to slow down growth; thought will, in the long run, be valued only by those who have been discouraged early from jumping at conclusions and from letting imagination run too far ahead of knowledge. But, here again, the danger lay in the existence of such a thing as a purely elementary education, not conceived as a preparation for any further stage of initiation into responsible thinking, and tending therefore to discharge youth into working life with no more than a child's thoughts and a child's knowledge.

The danger was increased, I thought, by the tendency, of this infantile bias to spread upwards into the Teachers' Training Colleges. It was for this reason that I rather discouraged the building of new colleges by local authorities and experimented with a scheme for bringing the existing non-university colleges into closer relation with the universities. That scheme was in operation for more than twenty years; but I cannot say that I found it very effective when, during the last half of its life, I came to operate it from the university end. In any case, the scheme has now been superseded and is not worth lingering over here, important though it seemed to me at the time.

It is in this setting of what was to prove the most stormy and fantastic era of modern history that the educational policies and controversies of the 'twenties are still, in some sort, alive and will have to be judged by historians. Of course, I cannot claim to have foreseen the burdens which the school generation of these days would have to bear; I can only claim to have been conscious of the general insecurity, moral and material, of the world into which it had been born. At least I hope I never wholly forgot what I had written in 1919, immediately after my Peace Conference experiences:

"If this was a war for national security and a stable balance of power, it has failed, for it has impoverished Western Europe and disintegrated Central and Eastern Europe and Western

Asia. If it was a war to make the world safe for democracy, it has failed, for the old ideas of constitutional democracy were never further from satisfying the desires of the peoples. If, finally, it was a war to end war, it has left the future of the world more uncertain and more contentious than at any period since the Reformation. . . . There is no rest for the generation that won the war; a vista of toil and self-abnegation lies before it."

CHAPTER VII

Indirect Rule in a Social Service 1924-9

In the last chapter, I have tried to view education in the 'twenties in the light of a lurid future; now, at the risk of being wearisome, I must try to view it in the light of the chief social problem of the 'twenties themselves: the all-pervading anxiety about employment. For the schools, the anxiety had two aspects: the dangers of juvenile unemployment or mis-employment for the school-leaver and the demoralizing effect on school children of life in a largely unemployed community. Both these problems were mainly regional problems; broadly speaking, they were serious only in what came to be known as the "depressed areas"; but they were none the less disturbing for that.

I

By far the less disturbing of the two was juvenile unemployment. On the whole, I think now that the government of 1924-9 had, little to reproach itself with in this field, and indeed that our anxieties about it, were unduly exaggerated. In June 1923, just before the first Baldwin Administration went hurriedly to the country and no less hurriedly vamped up for election purposes a programme of Instruction Centres for the juvenile unemployed, the number of girls and boys registered as unemployed exceeded 70,000. Two years earlier, at the time of the coal strike of 1921, it had been nearly 180,000. By contrast, even in June 1926, on the morrow of the General Strike and when the coal stoppage was still at its height, the figure rose only to 90,000; and, apart from that passing crisis, the figure fell fairly steadily to 51,000 in June 1929. This figure represented a rate of unemployment of hardly more than 3 per cent; and even in the black spot of Wales the rate was under 7 per cent. Moreover most of this unemployment was short-term; even in Wales five years later, when the situation was much worse, more than 70 per cent of the juveniles "on the register" had been unemployed for not more than three months; and the percentage for the whole country was about 80 per cent.[1] To some extent, this improvement over the period 1921–9 was due to a temporary decline in the numbers of the population between the ages of fourteen and eighteen; the census figure which had risen to a peak of 1,939,000 in 1921 had fallen by 1931 to 1,870,000. But to a large extent it was due also to greater efficiency in the working of the Juvenile Employment Exchanges. In 1921–2 they were placing actually fewer boys and girls under eighteen than they had placed in 1911, while in 1929 the number of placings had risen by more than 180 per cent.

My only part in this was an abdication. As the result of the report of the Malcolm Committee, I transferred the remnants of the Board of Education's responsibilities for juvenile employment to the Ministry of Labour. In this, I am sure I was right, though the step was resented by many "educationalists". It would have been right even if educational administrators and school teachers had been ideally wise; but, in fact, in those days the "elementary" branch of the teaching profession tended to suffer from a disturbing anti-employer complex, from which local Directors of Education also were not entirely immune. I remember, in my early days of office, preaching the gospel of co-operation with employers to a conference of teachers, only to be told afterwards by an elderly leader of the N.U.T. that he distrusted my views and would keep a sharp eye on my proceedings in future. In this complex, old prejudices, once not unjustified, against employers' methods of using juvenile labour were reinforced by the anti-vocational bias in educational thought to which I have already referred. A different kind of administration was needed to mediate between school and work.

This was the more necessary because the real problem of un-employment among the youth of the country was moving away

[1] These figures for the whole of Wales, of course, somewhat understate the gravity of the problem in the mining valleys.

from the doors of the elementary school, and had to be tackled as a "personnel" problem in industry itself. This was hardly recognized in the 'twenties, but it was to become startlingly evident in the 'thirties. It was no longer a question of finding jobs for elementary school leavers or even of guiding them away from "blind alley" employments. The deadly danger of the period was the insecurity of the skilled worker, not of the unskilled. The time was to come when, in an area of heavy industry like Tyneside, the blindest of all alleys was apprenticeship in shipbuilding or engineering: and when secondary schools and university alike had to contend against the instinct of the over-prudent parent to place his son at the earliest age in some modest job, offering no other prospect for the future than a reasonable immunity from the risks of industrial fluctuations. Secondary education was prized as a qualification for the more clerical of such jobs, but the aspirant to them must generally leave school at sixteen; for the longer he stayed, the nearer he approached to the dangerous age for employment which was tending to shift upwards to as high as twenty-one or twenty-two. The evil of educated unemployment never grew in this country to the dimensions which it assumed in Germany, where it became one of the main predetermining causes of Nazism; but it was dangerous enough in this country to discredit the schemes of educational reformers. I myself was always more anxious to revive Fisher's day continuation schools than to raise the school leaving age; but it became increasingly difficult to convince the sceptic of the relevance of even that proposal to the conditions of the day.

Outside the heavy industries day continuation schools would, indeed, have been relevant if they had been designed – as they specifically were not – to provide a remedy for the decay of apprenticeship training in industry, using the word "apprenticeship" broadly to describe due attention to the development of mind and skill in all young workers. Instead, the scheme of day continuation schools seemed to represent a renewal of the anti-vocational bias which had haunted even technical education itself from its original foundation by the Act of 1889. That Act had laid down that "the expression technical instruction shall mean instruction in the principles of science and art applicable to industries. *It shall not include teaching the practice of any trade or employment*". To eradicate the last remnants of this curious prejudice, and to re-plan technical education as an integral part of a progressive industrial training, was my main aim in this field, and on the whole the trend both of educational and industrial thought was in my favour; but, though the practice of the only day continuation school which had survived the Geddes axe, the school at Rugby, notably conformed to this general pattern, I could not contemplate with any enthusiasm the creation, at great expense, of a new form of part-time education which might, as a general rule, distract the attention of local education authorities away from the central need for improved vocational training. Indeed, the day continuation school idea had, from the beginning, been still-born owing to the anti-vocational bias of its midwives, and I doubt today whether the more ambitious County Colleges of the Butler Act will ever come to birth until they are more clearly envisaged as a supplement and auxiliary to the junior grades of the technical school.

2

So much for actual juvenile unemployment. But the effect of family unemployment upon the young in the depressed areas presented a much more serious problem and I do not think that the Baldwin administration can be acquitted of a certain insensitiveness to the magnitude and the intractibility of that problem, at any rate during its last two years in office when the dust of the coal strike had cleared away, leaving the main features of the social landscape to stand out in their uncompromising harshness.

For myself, I do not think that I shared this insensitiveness, for I saw too much of the facts; but, just because I saw the facts, I did take a somewhat defeatist view of the possible solutions of the problem. There were, basically, only two possible solutions: new industry or migration. They were not mutually exclusive, but I was

H

inclined to put the second first. To take the ugliest instance, life in the mining valleys of South Wales seemed to me to have been hopelessly disfigured by nearly eighty years of careless industrialism, from the time when imported Spanish workers had set the tone for a whole rabbit-warren of mean housing by digging themselves into the semi-subterranean dwellings of Dowlais. I could not believe in the possibility of any healthy revival on that spoilt ground, even if it should prove possible to attract new industries to the few remaining building sites in this countryside of steep hills and narrow levels. Time has, to some extent, proved me wrong and I blame myself for not having urged on my colleagues a more positive policy.

Not that I was alone in my defeatism. It is difficult for the citizens of the Welfare State in these 1950s to realize how slowly their pre-war predecessors, of all political complexions, rid themselves of the assumption that the movements of industry must necessarily be determined by solid economic motives and that the "artificial" attraction of new industries to depressed areas must therefore run counter to fundamental economic laws. Much later, in July 1935, Sir Malcolm Stewart, after six months' experience as Commissioner for the Special Areas of England and Wales, took the same defeatist view that I had taken more amateurishly eight years before. While he then recognized that "at once the most important and the most difficult of my duties" was to try to satisfy "the demand that something should be done to attract fresh industries" to these areas; he much more positively advised that "transference of individuals and families out of the Special Areas must in my view be regarded as one of the essential measures of relief". It was not till a year and a half later, in his report of November 1936, that he came to the conclusion "that *by means of state-provided inducements* a determined attempt should be made to attract industrialists to the Special Areas".

If I did not anticipate that conclusion in 1928; it was certainly not because I had any illusions about the difficulty of promoting migration, on any substantial scale, from the Welsh mining valleys. They had, indeed, as the no less depressed area of West

Durham had not, a long tradition of one kind of migration; they had made quite a business of sending girls straight from school into domestic service in England. But a pathetic attachment to the spoilt soil of the valleys was making even this a more distasteful adventure than formerly. One of these "tweenies" reported to her old headmistress about 1928, after her first year of service in a great country house, that she had hardly been able to bear it; it was a good household and both her employer and her fellow-servants had been kind, but she was "so frightened of the *anchestors* on the staircase". And for young men, migration away from their very real home culture, from the chapels and the adult schools and the choirs, seemed almost inconceivable except sometimes in groups to the new mining areas in Kent and South Yorkshire. I remember two charming unemployed young men who were offered good gardeners' jobs on a Wiltshire estate and who fled back to their derelict homes after one week's experience of life in a musicless English village. I soon grew to realize that these people really had something to be homesick for – that the tragedy of the valleys, far more than of West Durham or West Cumberland, was that they had so much of the materials for a healthy social life, if only they had not been left in a state of social segregation by the migration of their employers to the superior amenities of country houses in the vale of Glamorgan or farther afield. Even before the coal strike, the then president of the South Wales Miners' Federation said to me, as we drove past the almost abandoned steel works at Dowlais: "You know, I'm not a born Welshman and I feel no political bitterness; I do not blame the —— family for making money out of us in the past; but I cannot bear the thought that, having made it, they have gone away and left us to stew in our own juice."

But, after all, it was hardly the business of a Minister of Education to plan the movements of industry or of population; and I sank back, too contentedly perhaps, into a kind of benevolent slumming. I felt I could at least do something, under cover of inspecting subsiding school buildings or opening new technical schools or visiting new health clinics, to keep up the courage of almost hopless people by demonstrating that Whitehall had not wholly forgotten them.

Under that sort of cover, the first step towards encouragement was to ensure that school-children were at least decently well-fed. Here I nearly made a fatal mistake at the outset. My chief medical adviser, that great pioneer of health services, Sir George Newman, was beginning to retire a little into the false serenities of old age. He was impatient of a tendency among inexperienced local medical officers, with little knowledge of child health, to diagnose rickets on the most inadequate evidence; and he doubted the existence of any serious malnutrition in South Wales. I began by giving the House of Commons rather stilted assurances to this effect, thus provoking from Mr. Gerald Gould, I remember, the obvious, if slightly obtuse, retort that, "malnutrition" or no "malnutrition", these children were hungry. After my war contacts with Belgian relief, I knew at least that in the feeding of children more was required than a simple faith (to misquote Kipling) that "what Tommy needs is bulk in his inside". It was by no means children from the poorest homes who were the least well nourished; the greatest contrast was between the villages still inhabited by the old Welsh stock, with its sound tradition of family cookery, and those, usually lower down the valleys, which had been occupied, in the course of years, by what were locally known as "Bristolians", the mixed overspill of the neighbouring docks, with no tradition beyond fish and chips. I hope I shall not be accused of colour consciousness if I say that one knew at once which sort of village one was in by the presence or absence of "blackamoor" children in the school.

Moreover, the food at canteens organized by voluntary effort was not always as good as the children could find at home. When I ordered a special investigation, the investigating medical officer was almost equally shocked by the indubitable existence of a substantial number of under-nourished children and by the clumsiness of some such canteens where children were being fed, as I myself saw on one visit to a church hall in Monmouthshire, exclusively on corned beef sandwiches out of tins, without a trace of greenstuff, not even a cabbage leaf. Nor was it only volunteer helpers who made this elementary dietetic mistake – or had some excuse for making it. I remember calling at this time for the Guardians' lists of foodstuffs obtainable by families on poor relief in the county of Durham. When I remonstrated that the lists contained no green vegetables at all, unless tinned sweet corn could be dignified by that name, I was told, not quite truly, that there *were* no green vegetables in County Durham, except prize leeks which, being grown for size, had, with some justice, ceased to be regarded locally as food at all.

The difficulty about providing free school meals at the expense of the rates was never frankly stated, because I could not decently say in public what chairmen of education committees told me in private. The truth was that local Labour councillors dared not put into force the clause in the Education Act instituting free meals for children whose families could not afford to feed them adequately, because they did not trust their fellow councillors to resist local pressure to extend such meals indiscriminately. In the House of Commons I was often pressed to transfer the cost of free meals from rates to taxes, by making special grants to impoverished local authorities; but I do not remember receiving, publicly or privately, any representations of this kind from local authorities themselves. The leaders of such authorities, not least those belonging to the Labour party, had a high sense of administrative integrity and they feared an epidemic of cadging even more than a new burden on the rates. I often urged them to imitate the London County Council which had long ago hit on the expedient of keeping the relevant clause in the Education Act permanently in force, but using it only for supplying free milk and cod-liver oil to selected children recommended by the school doctor. Future progress was, in fact, to lie in this direction, until the present system of almost universal school meals developed after World War II; but, at the time, it seemed to local authorities, not unnaturally, to be an invitation to make the worst of both worlds; for, if they distrusted their ability to hold the door against the cadgers, it seemed folly to begin by half opening it. In these

circumstances, a more or less effective defence against under-
nourishment had to be provided mainly by voluntary effort –
mainly, because not all local authorities persisted in the attitude I
have described, I blame myself now, not so much for failing to
deal more drastically with the problem as it then existed, which as
yet hardly constituted a serious threat to public health, but rather
for failing to plan machinery which would have been adequate to
meet the much more serious situation which was to develop in the
thirties.

At this earlier stage of "depression" boots were, indeed, a more
obvious problem than food. Here, I resorted more directly and
personally to a form of voluntary relief in South Wales, administered as quietly and informally as possible, through head
teachers or Directors of Education. My aim was to demonstrate
how simply – and cheaply – the need could be, at least temporarily,
met if it were kept outside the range of official policies and political
pressures. There remains with me the picture of a steep street in
Rhymney with a little boy clattering happily down it in clogs –
but he was the son of the bank manager and the only boy in the
town, so the head master told me, to whom shoe-leather was not
the indispensable mark of social respectability.

If anyone had told me at the time, what no doubt many thought,
that this personal slumming was beneath the dignity of a Minister
whose business should have been to devise policy in Whitehall, I
should have resented the criticism. So long as Whitehall and
Westminster continued in the old manner to rely for the provision
of employment and the relief of distress upon the economic
impulses of free enterprise and the administrative responsibility of
local authorities, it was above all things necessary to hearten by
one's personal presence local authorities whom economic impulses
had left in the lurch. After all, these people were in a state of siege
and if no one thought it possible to raise the siege, the least one
could do was to hearten the garrison. But my critics would have
been right from the point of view of party political prudence. A
Minister cannot interest himself in the relief of distress, however
quietly, without advertising its existence and, if he relies for

relief on voluntary effort, he can set no limits to the enthusiasm of his volunteers. And so, in the winter of 1928-9, with a General Election in immediate prospect, I found myself not only involved in, but reluctantly responsible for, a Lord Mayor's Fund for the relief of the depressed areas and a full-dress publicity campaign for subscriptions to it, with all the dramatizations incidental to such a campaign – all of them eminently quotable by political opponents. The Chancellor of the Exchequer was violently annoyed by this publicity, but he was himself partly responsible for its loudness; for he had rejected my plea for a single initial government grant to the fund and had insisted on contributing only pound for pound. Desiring thus to stimulate private giving, he could not justly complain of the methods inseparable from such stimulation. Neville Chamberlain was better entitled to complain, but he did not complain so openly. Indeed, he surprised me by his encouragement when the Fund was first launched; but as the publicity developed, and as the money began to be spent, not always judiciously, he found, I think, new reasons for distrusting my "drive". How far the expenditure of the Fund did any permanent good, or how far it opened the door to the cadgers, I am in no position to judge, for I left office too soon after the organization I started had got to work; certainly the episode did no good to me.

3

No doubt it was the Mr. Darcy in me that so much preferred this direct touch with the personalities of local administration to the generalized debates of the House of Commons. I remember many such debates on the Education Estimates, both while I was in office and before and since; but none that seemed to me to be worthy of the subject. And I do not think I felt this merely because I was a bad "House of Commons man".

The chief lurking problem in an English parliamentary Welfare State is that the House of Commons is, on the whole, so good a judge of administration conducted in the grand manner, by broad categories, "with vision" as the modern cant term goes, but on the whole so bad a one of what I may call "pastoral" administration: the application of administration to the bodies and minds of the individual citizen. Bad, because it knows that this kind of administration is not its business. The reformed House of Commons of 1832 had to learn laboriously, over a difficult century, to keep clear of all those spheres of administration into which personal patronage may most easily and most disastrously intrude, whether it be the internal discipline of the Services of the Crown, civil or military, or the discretionary assistance given by the State, within broad statutory limits, to individual citizens through "social services". In the Crown Services we may be thankful that the lesson has been so well learned; and, remembering an unhappy phase of Army administration in 1938-9, we may above all be thankful that it has been learnt by Ministers as well as by Members of Parliament. In that field there is little place for the short cuts of administration by personal touch. But in the social services, effective administration stands or falls by the saving grace of neighbourliness. That grace does save local administration, even when, as sometimes, the temptations of local politics turn it sour; and if, as seems inevitable nowadays, these services must grow more centralized as their scope expands beyond municipal capacities, that same grace must somehow find its way through the screen of faithful civil servants, advisory boards and doubtfully representative professional associations, behind which a Minister in Whitehall is perforce condemned to operate. If it does not get through, what happens may be seen, as I write, in the expanding universe of the National Health service, where a central administration, quite remarkably sensitive, on the whole, to the humanities of its task, yet seems to swing in an ever remoter orbit round the personal doctor-patient relationship, on which all else depends. Or so, at least, both the doctor and the patient tend increasingly to feel.

In my day, the trend of educational administration was mercifully rather in the reverse direction. It had started, after the Act of 1902, under the dictatorial hand of Sir Robert Morant, as a highly centralized system devised to keep a new breed of local authorities under the close control of the Wise Men of Whitehall. That may have been necessary in those pioneering days, though I cannot help thinking that Morant corrupted the Board's official English for a generation by a monumental "code" of statutory regulations whose main purpose was to invest the Board, by the deliberate use of ambiguous language, with more powers than Parliament had ever intended to give it. But by 1924 the Board had already gone far to emancipate local authorities from such detailed control; the inspectorate was settling down to act rather as advisors to authorities and teachers than as laborious inquisitors of individual schools: and the "code" had long become out of date. I took pleasure in adding a few finishing touches to this emancipation; in reducing the "code" to reasonable size and intelligible language and in abolishing formal inspection of elementary education, school by school. But this trend was introducing a new danger: that educational policy might in practice be worked out, not by personal touch with a diversity of local authorities, but by negotiations with a national Association of Education Committees managed by a small group of experienced Councillors and Directors of Education, with its own weekly journal, its own Members of Parliament, and its own alliances or feuds with an even more highly-centralized National Union of Teachers. The densest screen that can shut out Whitehall from real tactical control of a social service – far denser than any General Staff of civil servants – is a screen composed of persons elected by elected persons, for the graces of representative government cannot be transmitted at second hand.

I say that this was the danger; but when I tried to get behind that screen, I found it easy, for the local Nestors of education who composed it – with the exception, perhaps, of one or two of the harder-bitten Directors of Education – were as much on their guard as I could be against the temptation to play at caucus politics. Chief among them were two men whom I should have liked to exhibit to the world as representing the best in English local government: George Lunn of Newcastle, all evangelical fire yet always at home with children, and Percy Jackson of the West Riding, all solid Yorkshire common sense; both Free Church liberal veterans of the struggle against the Act of 1902, who had sworn, since the war, to fight no more over education (so long, at least, as the President of the Board was not too unreasonable). Perhaps that vow had hardly been taken by their chief professional henchman in the Association of Education Committees, Percival Sharp, the Director of Education for Sheffield, a little combative bull-terrier of a man, a supremely able organizer who had, however, come to the top the hard way and seemed to me to look at education always rather from the extinct pupil-teacher's point of view. He and I might well have quarrelled; but we happened to like each other and, from his point of view, he was no doubt kinder to me than I deserved. Not unlike Lunn and Jackson, but with a very different background, was the Labour Chairman of the Glamorgan Education Committee, William Jenkins, a silent member of Parliament but a statesman in his native hills, who showed me the mining valleys and, while encouraging me to run free in them, stood always ready with wise advice, salted by an inimitable chuckle of humour. Along with these, my memory wanders through a whole portrait gallery of local worthies who took little part in Whitehall negotiations but gave themselves to the cultivation of their own gardens, from Quiller-Couch, pawkily coaxing the farmers of Cornwall, who admired education but did not love their rates, to that model Kentish partnership of squire, magnate and scholar, Mark Collet, Lord Sackville and their Director, Salter-Davies, who made their difficult mixed county a pattern for the nation.

I could prolong this list indefinitely, but the longer I made it, the more invidious would be the inevitable omissions. My object has been only to convey the flavour of my work in these five years and to explain why I found such pleasure in it. In this kind of administration one always hopes (though it may be a pathetic illusion) that one's most lasting achievements are not the ideas one tries actively to popularize or impose, but those that grow, as it were, under one's feet. I had, for instance, to walk very gingerly in the whole field of religious education; there, feelings were still just touchy enough to defeat my attempts to work out the terms of an "enabling bill" which might give a little more flexibility to permissible local arrangements between local authorities and religious bodies. But I was known to feel strongly on the subject and to take a somewhat supersectarian view of it (if that word be allowable): and, though I took no direct part in the movement towards "agreed syllabuses" of religious instruction and agreed forms of school worship, I like to think that the extraordinary development of that movement in my time owed something to my influence.

This method of administration by "indirect rule" – a rule as indirect as any that Lugard invented for African territories – was, of course, even more applicable to teachers than to local authorities. Over local authorities one had a majestic statutory authority, when one wished to use it; but over teachers in their schools, one had practically no authority at all. Constitutionally they were the servants of the local authorities, not of the State; and traditionally, they were free to teach as they pleased. The link between them and the Board was the body of H.M. Inspectors; and both inspectors and teachers shared a kind of independence which seems to come into being only under British rule: an independence of *moral*, hardly safeguarded by any constitutional guarantees. This gave to my contacts with the teaching profession, in local conferences and in the summer courses held annually at Oxford and Cambridge, a freedom of discussion which taught me much and teachers perhaps a little.

But if, as I think, something like this indirect rule is the necessary pattern of all social service administration, it is not one to be recommended to an ambitious politician. A Minister who thus, in the French phrase, *paye de sa personne* in a particular field is apt to find himself tethered there. Not that I ever thought of "promotion" during these five years; but I got a slight shock when Baldwin told me that he would expect me to remain at the Board if his government were returned at the General Election of 1929 – until I moved out of home politics altogether, of which alternative I shall have something to say later. There may be a serious problem here for the future administration of social services in a Welfare State.

CHAPTER VIII

Baldwin in Power

I

If I pause at the watershed of 1929 to look back over the first ten years of the Twenty Years' Truce, my survey will be frankly an exercise in hindsight. I have already written of the Peace Conference and the later days of the Lloyd George régime; my theme must now be the first seven years of Baldwin as a national figure, from the Carlton Club meeting to the General Election which ended his second administration. I do not claim to have thought at the time the thoughts that I now record. Some of them I did think then, but I should be afraid to pick these out at this distance of time; it seems better to record them all as wisdom after the event. To tell the truth, I seldom concerned myself actively in matters outside my own departmental duties and I have never had much faith in my current judgments on issues with which I have no direct administrative touch.

This confession raises, of course, the old question whether a Cabinet ought to contain a medley of departmentally pre-occupied Ministers, or whether it should be confined to half-a-dozen overlords, accustomed to think in terms of ends rather than of means and able to issue broad directives of policy to which departmental ministers outside the Cabinet should be expected to conform. The Bonar Law and Baldwin Cabinets were a more or less conscious return to the traditional system, after Lloyd George's experiments in various kinds and degrees of overlordship. My own view has always been that no Cabinet can be trusted which does not consist mainly of Ministers responsible for departmental administration. Cabinet Ministers must not only have "time to think"; they must also have food for responsible thought; nor can decisions on policy be effectively conveyed to departments through the medium of impersonal Cabinet minutes. But departmental responsibility could in theory, be reconciled with a quite small Cabinet if departments were grouped under Cabinet Ministers, each with his own sub-Cabinet, as it were, of departmental Ministers, over whom he exercised a real superintendence. There are, however, two practical difficulties about this idea. The lesser of the two is the one that sprang at once to the mind of Baldwin, the party manager, when one tried the idea on him: that, at any rate during the transition when the scheme was being put into operation, it would not offer a sufficient number of "plums" for aspiring members of Parliament who would not be content with what would seem relegation to a mere Second Eleven – and a discontented Second Eleven would be strong enough to ruin the *moral* of a government. The greater difficulty is that, if such grouping were to be a reality, it would have to be geographical, including a comprehensive re-planning of departmental buildings. Superintendence would be a fiction, and would become a mere nuisance, if superintending Ministers had to follow their scattered flocks over all the area from Whitehall to Blackfriars and Mayfair. It was on this rock, I think, that Churchill's rather half-hearted experiment in overlordship in his last administration foundered; and I doubt whether the Ministry of Defence will become an administrative reality until the geographical problem has been better solved.

Anyway, the traditional system of large comprehensive Cabinets has the virtue of making the constitutional doctrine of corporate Cabinet responsibility a reality and it works better in normal times than might be expected. No Cabinet, large or small can originate policy; initiative must always lie with individual Ministers. There is always, too, in practice, an inner Cabinet, however informal, whose members determine major policies, and minor issues are commonly referred to Cabinet Committees. In the years 1924-9 I remember, of course, many occasions when a policy thus worked out was discussed and accepted by the full Cabinet; but none when the discussion, taken by itself, could be regarded as adequate, and only one when the Cabinet rejected a strong recommendation by the responsible Minister – and that was a recommendation, at short notice, that it should modify a policy already adopted on the Minister's recommendation. The Cabinet of 1924–9 was, no doubt, an exceptionally harmonious one and its harmony was favoured by what I take to have been a traditional practice, now tending to fall into disuse; the practice of full and rounded oral dissertations by the Foreign Secretary and the Chancellor of the Exchequer. That practice sometimes irked me, for these dissertations occupied almost the first half of every regular Cabinet meeting; but they had the immense advantage of acquainting the full Cabinet, well in advance of proposals for action, with the trend of the Minister's mind. If, as I imagine, that practice has given place to what may appear to be more "business-like" discussions, the loss is great; statesmanship is essentially different from business and requires its own technique; but already, in those days, only Austen Chamberlain, Churchill and, during the short time left to him, Curzon had inherited the art of such dissertations, while newer men with broad views on policy, like Amery, tended to rely on the method of written memoranda, which, while appearing to save Cabinet time, failed usually to capture the attention of its members.

The Cabinet of 1924–9 was, of course, fortunate in two respects. For one thing, it had hardly ever to deal with a sudden emergency, for which its mind had not been prepared in advance, or with an issue of policy for which no single Minister was responsible and which no "inner Cabinet" had prepared for its consideration. When it did find itself in this position, as when the Naval Conference at Geneva was on the verge of breakdown or when it attempted to tackle the problem of House of Lords reform, it worked clumsily, though I doubt whether a smaller Cabinet would have worked much better in the circumstances. Its other good fortune was that the growing tendency of the Chancellor of the Exchequer to censor in advance all Cabinet business which might trench on financial policy had not yet encroached seriously on the initiative of other Ministers or on the freedom of Cabinet

deliberations. When it did so later in the hands of Neville
Chamberlain, the argument for a small Cabinet of very senior
Ministers became stronger, because this sort of Treasury veto
could be effectively challenged only in an intimate body of equals,
where a Prime Minister, a Foreign Secretary, a Defence Minister
and a Minister-in-Chief for the Social Services would carry equal
weight with a Chancellor of the Exchequer, without risking an
open disagreement which might split a government.

The reader between the lines will discern that this is the picture
of a Cabinet not dominated by a strong Prime Minister. That is
true. I do not know what part Baldwin took in "inner" discussions
with his senior colleagues; but in the full Cabinet he was content
to act as an indulgent chairman, letting its members have their
head but rarely giving them a lead. The odd thing is that, nevertheless, it was, from first to last, unmistakably a Baldwin Cabinet.
To explain this, future historians will have to draw a fuller portrait
of Baldwin than they will find in most of the studies of him that
have hitherto been published. By far the best of these studies is his
son's; but it is predominantly a study of personal character and
needs to be supplemented by a companion portrait of the statesman in action. And his portrait in that capacity has usually been
drawn too much against the background of the years 1931-7; the
years of what may fairly be called his Great Administration, have
been too much neglected. I am no portrait-painter on this scale;
but I must try, at this point, to add a few touches to the sketch of
him which I began two chapters ago.

2

It follows from what I have already said that Baldwin cared
greatly for the *tone* of government, but for particular measures of
policy only as they were needed to set and keep up that tone. It
was, I confess, this mind in him that attracted me to him when I
first entered Parliament and when he was hardly more than an
obscure newcomer in Lloyd George's last Cabinet. At that time,
after all the stridencies and the varied policy-mongering of the

years since the Armistice, tone seemed to me to be the one thing in politics that really mattered. And in 1924–9 it still seemed to me to be the thing that mattered most. The task of this second Baldwin Government, both at home and abroad, was stabilization and settlement – or, in Baldwin's own words written long afterwards, "the healing of the nation". To that end Baldwin had succeeded in re-uniting his party in a Cabinet some of whose most experienced members had bitterly resented, and indeed despised, the part he had played in the previous two years. That achievement should not be underrated; Birkenhead, who had perhaps felt more resentment and contempt than the others, paid a touching tribute to it in his brief farewell to the Cabinet on his resignation at the end of 1928. And if no one but Baldwin could have achieved the initial reconciliation; he alone, I think, could have held this mixed company together in such good-feeling for nearly five years, by his curious gift of unobtrusive moral authority. This reunion gave him, on the whole, an effective administrative team, including, in the two Chamberlains, at least two colleagues on whom he could rely for the initiation and execution of large, if cautious, policies, abroad and at home. He supported both, loyally and, on the whole, understandingly; and his support contributed more, probably, to their very solid achievements than any attempt he could have made to alloy their policies with bright ideas of his own, in the Lloyd George manner. In general, it would almost be true to say that he trusted his colleagues for all executive action and himself only for expounding their policies to the country in terms which public opinion would understand and approve. That could not, of course, be wholly true, for he could not carry the responsibility for exposition unless he carried also some responsibility for modulating the policies he was to expound; but, subject to that inevitable reservation, he was, I think, all too content to regard himself as the mouthpiece of his government, rather than as its directing brain.

Too content – yet that is, after all, the principal part which leaders of parliamentary democracies have always played – and never more significantly so than since the advent of universal suffrage. Few peace-time Prime Ministers and still fewer Presidents of the United States are remembered by posterity for their measures; most are remembered, if at all, for trends of political thought and behaviour which they have set in motion or of which they have made themselves the recognized exponents. Among Baldwin's own contemporaries, that had been true of Theodore Roosevelt, his senior by less than ten years, and of Lloyd George, his senior by less than five, for all the administrative energy they had seemed to radiate. Among the great figures of the nineteenth century, Peel and Disraeli are perhaps the only ones who may be remembered chiefly for their measures; Gladstone is alive today, not so much as the great free-trade Chancellor of the Exchequer or as the author of compulsory education and the Civil Service, but rather as the prophet of the Midlothian Campaign. The same, I think, is true even of the younger Pitt who before 1793 had already changed the face and temper of parliamentary government, not by the infusion of new policies, but by the mere impression of a monumental personality. That was Balfour's meaning when after Baldwin's first big speech on India in November 1929, he wrote to him, almost from his death-bed, that "no more can be given even to those who are greedy of posthumous fame" than to have worthily "treated the greatest of political themes" in parliamentary debate.

Unfortunately for Baldwin, these victories of personality must be won at a price, which he was hardly self-assertive enough to pay. The moral leader must occupy the whole stage of public life, pushing into the background his fellow-actors whose voices might jar with his. Or else, he must be blessed with colleagues who will take their cue wholly from him. On the whole, Baldwin was thus blessed in the administration of 1924–9; there were few voices in that cast to compete with his; in their widely different ways, Austen Chamberlain's grand manner in foreign policy and Balfour's delicacy of touch in drafting the report of the Imperial Conference of 1926, chimed well enough with his thought; in comparison with them, the wrong notes that I, for instance, struck in educational administration mattered little, nor the

I

periodical clatter at the back of the stage which Sir Alan Herbert
unkindly immortalized in his reference to

> "The gentle sound of dropping bricks –
> Will no one silence Auntie Jix?"

Yet Baldwin was, on occasion, oddly careless of the risks he ran in
handing a megaphone to the wrong member of the cast, though,
more usually, he exaggerated the risks of giving even the smaller
parts in the play to untried actors. For instance, on the one hand,
in the General Strike he encouraged Churchill to create and edit
the *British Gazette*, in order, so he told me pawkily, to keep him
occupied; and he remained apparently so insensitive to the in-
appropriateness of the tone to which that journal had set government policy that, a few months later, he left Churchill, cheerfully
enough, to handle the Coal Strike while he took his annual holiday
abroad. Yet, on the other hand, anxious though I know him to
have been in 1924, to give at least subordinate office to some
of the younger members of his party, he missed in the next five
years more than one opportunity of recruiting outstanding
parliamentarians like Macmillan and Oliver Stanley – not on
personal grounds, but, principally, I think, from a doubt whether
(so to speak) they would sing in tune. From the first of these
instances, one would have thought he had no ear; from the
second, that he was determined to sing solo and wanted no
accompaniment. Both judgments would have been wrong; but
(to change the metaphor) it must be admitted that he was too
loyal to the older hounds in his pack to whip them off when they
occasionally ran riot and too negligent about ensuring a young
entry. Consequently, when he retired in 1937, he left behind him
a tradition but no school; and this failure was not wholly due to
his entanglement during the last six years of his active life in the
complications of successive coalitions. In spite of the very real
affection which he had inspired, there was no group of "Mr. Pitt's
young men" to carry on the tradition – but then, he might have
said, most of Mr. Pitt's young men did not stand the test of time,
and he could never have got on with Canning.

It is partly the puzzle presented by these contradictory negligences that has led so many commentators to envelope Baldwin in the easy blanket explanation that he was just plain lazy. That will not do; he was habitually a far harder worker than most of his contemporaries; he had need to be, for he had neither Balfour's quickness of intellect, nor Churchill's versatility. But he had all the hermit-crab's apparatus for retiring into his shell in face of irrelevant importunities or of problems not yet ripe for solution. That, however, was no more than the self-protective mechanism which all highly-strung men have to evolve if they are to survive the strains of public responsibility. Evasiveness is the commonest charge brought in these days against all statesmen: in Geoffrey Dawson's diaries, for instance, against both Lloyd George and Baldwin in turn; by Bonar Law's biographer, Robert Blake, against Asquith; by Garvin against Gladstone's dealings with Joseph Chamberlain. The awkward feature of Baldwin's evasions was his apparently eccentric judgment of which things really mattered and which had better, for the moment, be allowed to take their own course. He kept his eye on the ball all right; but too often it seemed to be the ball on the next tee but two. The middle distance is not a good focus for the political golfer; it inevitably makes him a careless putter.

This peculiarity became obvious enough after the fall of his second administration; from 1929 onwards his mind was not really on the economic crisis nor on Empire preference, nor even on his fight with the Press barons; it was already on India, and in certain moods he would talk in private about nothing else. What is not so obvious, and seems to have escaped everyone's attention, is that, even during his Great Administration, he was already overwhelmingly preoccupied with the problem of the Prince of Wales. The most eccentric act of his whole public life was surely his determination, in the late summer of 1927, to leave a deeply divided Cabinet to clear up the wreckage of the Geneva Conference while he accompanied the Prince to Canada. Undoubtedly he overrated both his influence with the Prince and the opportunities of influence which this voyage would offer him;

but, undoubtedly too, the Prince, with his usual charm, had given him some cause to miscalculate thus. We are here in a region of personal relationships, where the truth could be known only to two people and will now probably never be known to anyone else, owing to the loyal reticence of one of the actors and the bad memory of the other; but no one who was at all in Baldwin's confidence at the time could mistake either his deep anxiety about the problem or his sense of personal responsibility for averting the danger that he foresaw. He failed to avert it, but, when it came in 1936, he was at least prepared for it and his manner of dealing with it would have been less sure if he had not brooded over it so far in advance of its coming.

On the whole, I think this middle-sightedness will stand the test of ultimate history pretty well. Baldwin was right, though riskily right, in thinking that, in day-to-day politics, false moves can be corrected at slight cost, provided only that they are honest. The truculence of the *British Gazette* was soon forgotten and, in itself, left few scars; its only effect on history, as it is being written today, has been to foster the myth of a divided Cabinet during the General Strike, split between mild Baldwinites and a ginger group, pressing for stronger action. So too with House of Lords reform; the only effect of that experimental testing of public opinion (for it was thus that Baldwin regarded it, no doubt too lightly) has been to prompt Mr. G. M. Young's slightly ill-natured guess that Baldwin must have lost control of his Cabinet. And Baldwin cared nothing for any judgment of history passed within twenty years of the event. Similarly, when I got into my mess in 1926, he quite light-heartedly told me that we must pay the price of convincing an ex-Liberal like Churchill that the Conservative party really cared about education. Here, too, he was right, for the deserved unpopularity incurred by this hit-and-miss economy campaign, not only in education, faded quickly, and the blunder, such as it was, was retrieved without much difficulty. On the other hand, ultimate history may not judge this middle-sightedness so kindly in the sphere of foreign policy. There, false moves in the immediate present cannot be retrieved so cheaply, nor is middle-

sightedness any substitute for far-sightedness. And to real far-
sightedness, the telescopic vision that is the rarest of political
virtues, Baldwin would have made no claim for himself.

It is only in this sense that the common gibe is true, that Baldwin
did not understand foreign policy or care much for it. In truth, he
was much less insular-minded than Edward Grey had been;
perhaps it would have been well if he had been more so. Almost
on our first acquaintance, at a moment when he was much moved
by the return of his son Oliver from a Russian prison, he let fall
the remark that he had only one ideal in foreign policy: to be a
"good European". There lay his weakness, for he was soon to
find – and was too much of a realist not to recognize – that, in his
sense, there were hardly any good Europeans left in Europe. That
being so, he constantly brooded over the dilemma which he was
shrewd enough to see more clearly than most of his contemporaries: that, in the absence of good Europeans, the League of
Nations must have some powers of coercion, but that such powers
as had been proposed in Macdonald's Geneva "Protocol" of 1924
could be entrusted only to good Europeans, while the powers of
coercion by economic boycott provided by the Covenant could
not be used effectively, or even safely, by a League which did not
include the United States. The wildest misjudgment of the Baldwin of the 'thirties is that he fell a victim, with so many of his
contemporaries, to the myth of "collective security". He never
did; but I am afraid he eventually made the mistake, in the
Abyssinian crisis, of thinking he could convince his countrymen
of the weakness of collective security by "trying it out", without
incurring any more serious penalties than he would have suffered –
and had suffered on more than one occasion – by a similar doubtful move in domestic politics.

This, however, is to run ahead of my story, which is of the
Baldwin of 1924–9. In that period, the policy of the Foreign
Office suited his middle-sightedness admirably: to make the
League of Nations work for all it was worth, but for no more; to
supplement it by limited regional commitments, rather than by
unlimited "global" ones; and, as Austen Chamberlain once ex-

pressed it, to keep in step with France while conducting an orderly retreat from the Peace of Versailles.

3

But the legend of Baldwin's indolence has arisen, not only from his middle-sightedness, but even more from his refusal to fiddle with problems before they were ripe for solution. This capacity for holding one's hand is a valuable quality of statesmanship; but in certain circumstances it is easily mistaken for helplessness. To take the crucial instance: was Baldwin's failure to end the coal stoppage by agreement after the termination of the General Strike in May 1926 an instance of helplessness? He had asked the nation, in his famous broadcast, to trust him to see justice done and he set out with the greatest determination to fulfil this promise on May 14, even before the aftermath of the General Strike had been cleared up; but did he not allow himself to be rebuffed too easily by both miners and employers and to acquiesce too lightly in the prolongation of the stoppage by eight dreary months? I doubt it; and I think history will doubt it. Of course, Baldwin was not a resourceful negotiator – nor for that matter, was Churchill; but his promise to the T.U.C. at the close of the General Strike was to "do all I can to ensure a just and lasting settlement"; and such a settlement is seldom secured by diplomatic ingenuities. Subsequent developments in the mining industry have served to emphasize that a lasting settlement could be based only upon the real solvency of the industry, which even ten years of nationalization have as yet been unable to secure for it. Even the suspension of the seven-hour day, so bitterly resented at the time, looks more reasonable in the light of the nationalized industry's struggle for increased productivity twenty years later. Even the principle of district, as against national, agreements was arguably sound, however stupid might be the bad manners of the employers in insisting upon it; for both sides in the industry had sufficiently demonstrated their inability to evolve reasonable leadership at the national level. "Reorganization" – if that shadowy catchword had any real substance in it – was certainly a matter for district administration. There was at least enough in these considerations, right or wrong, to persuade Baldwin that the time was not ripe for any agreed settlement and that the fire must be allowed to burn itself out.

But of one thing I am sure: Baldwin's choice of this policy was deliberate and was in no sense the easy refuge of an indolent man. In the midnight Cabinet meeting on May 2, he was not overruled by any "wild men" among his colleagues; none of them felt more strongly than he the essentially revolutionary situation created by the strike notices and the danger of negotiating under such a threat. But as the meeting was breaking up, he said aside to me: "Oh Eustace, I did not sign on for this." From that hour, except for one moment of elation nine days later, when the General Strike ended, the remainder of the year was for him, I think, a continuous agony of disappointment and responsibility; and the worst of the agony was to sit still and keep his temper.

Yet, in the end, judging the state of the nation in January 1927 by his unvarying moral standard, he might well have congratulated himself on his patience. It is extraordinary how little bitterness the slow crumbling of the strike had left behind it. On the whole, T.U.C. and miners alike had learnt to blame themselves; and if the mine owners had not yet learnt that lesson, a new generation of employer-technicians was growing up with a better capacity for self-criticism. Miss Bondfield's courage in signing the report of the Blanesburgh Committee on Unemployment Insurance seemed to be an earnest of a change of temper. The Government itself seemed as robust as it had been in its first year of office; the initiative in industrial reconstruction which it had lost in 1926, it seemed to regain at this moment by the Electricity Act, for which Baldwin might well claim personal credit, for, unexpectedly enough, it was the only piece of legislation in which I remember him taking a keen personal interest; abroad, Germany's admission to the League of Nations with a permanent seat on the Council, had at last been accomplished, and British intervention in China bade fair to open a better phase, though an only too brief one, in a problem which had been one of the chief headaches of foreign policy for the past three years. But why then did Baldwin allow his Cabinet, in the following May, to revive all the dying bitternesses of 1926 by the Trades Disputes Act?

This bids fair to become, in some quarters, the chief count in the indictment against Baldwin for a certain half-indolent weakness. But, here again, I do not think the charge does much credit to the critics' imagination. It is true that he would have preferred to introduce no legislation at all; but it is also true that to characterize the Bill whose introduction he actually approved as, in Wickham Steed's words, "blatantly reactionary" is simply silly. Apart from the old issue of the political levy, it confined itself to the out-lawry of certain characteristic features of the political legend of the "general strike", as it had been evolved by Sorel for revolutionary purposes before 1914 and had haunted the left wing of European and even American trade unionism ever since the war. But "haunted" is the right word; this was a myth which excited men or terrified them only until an attempt was made to translate it into action; one touch of experience was enough to lay the turnip-ghost. And in England it had been laid; to bury the frag-ments of the bogey solemnly with bell, book and candle was just childish. That was the real argument against legislation; but it was not the sort of argument that occurs naturally to the citizens of a parliamentary democracy when they have been frightened. What commentators forget is that ordinary citizens had been profoundly frightened, not only in 1926, but at least ever since the "Council of Action" in 1920; and it was not unnatural for them to ask for some guarantee that they would not be so frightened again. Of all human virtues, generosity is the most individual and the hardest to translate into corporate terms. I have little doubt that Baldwin could have argued the nation into generosity in 1927; but the argument, if honestly developed, would have involved the use of language, about the Labour leaders' rashness in playing with fire for six years till they burned their fingers in 1926, which would have been hardly less wound-ing than the terms of an Act of Parliament. For, after all, no worse insult can be offered to any man than an ostentatious generosity.

Baldwin's instinct was simply to forget; but it was obvious enough, even to colleagues who most completely shared his instinct, that, as a matter of practical politics, mere forgetfulness "would not do". And Baldwin was shrewd enough to reach the same conclusion, and to content himself with an Act which, if his instinct was right, would be almost completely inoperative – as in fact it was.

There remains the more formidable criticism that Baldwin remained culpably inactive during the last two years of his administration in face of the problem of unemployment. The Trade Disputes Act in the summer of 1927 and the Unemployment Insurance Act in the autumn absorbed too much Parliamentary time, and, in the interval, the disaster of the Geneva Conference had damaged the Government's reputation almost past repair. Yet, so it is said, he took no steps to repair it, either by taking the opportunity of Robert Cecil's resignation in October to reconstruct his Cabinet or by launching any new line of policy. True, a government which enacts, in its last year of office, as this government did in 1928, a large extension of the franchise and a comprehensive reconstruction of local government, including a drastic relief of industry from the burden of local taxation and a large advance in the direction of the break-up of the Poor Law, cannot fairly be called inactive: but in face of rising unemployment and the continuing weakness of the steel and coal industries, were these cumbrous measures any evidence of the sort of activity which the country looked for on the eve of a General Election?

I think that, at the end of 1927, Baldwin did make one miscalculation. "Safety First" was not his invention as an election slogan, for he did not think in slogans; but it fitted, not too badly, his instinct at this time. He would not have put it in Churchill's dramatic terms in the Budget speech of 1929: "better hard times and a continuing nation than lush, lavish indulgence and irrevocable decline" – for neither did he think in dramatic alternatives. But he had a sense of approaching danger, typified to him by the growing recklessness of American economic practice. What could one hope of capitalism or the gold standard, if these were the practices of their chief exponents? So far, he certainly did not miscalculate; but he may well have misjudged the prospects of Britain's "natural" recovery. He still held the opinion, expressed in his Plymouth speech in October 1923, that the "unemployment problem is the most crucial problem of our country. I can fight it. I cannot fight it without weapons. The only way of fighting this subject is by protecting the home market." But since that weapon had been denied him, will the delay from 1928 until, say, 1932 when the iron and steel industry began to be reorganized under the shelter of a tariff wall, bulk so large in the perspective of history? And could Baldwin be blamed if, meanwhile, he congratulated himself, at the end of 1927, on the improvement which then seemed to be taking place in the country's economy? Unemployment figures, which had stood at over 1,450 in December 1922 and had fallen beneath the million mark in the week before the General Strike, now stood at just under 1,200: the cost of living was steadily falling; money wages were being stabilized and real wages rising; the country's favourable balance of trade had been larger in 1927 than in 1924 and was to rise still further in 1928 to more than two-thirds of the pre-war figure. But in fact, the signs of recovery in the level of unemployment were to prove illusory; in that respect, the state of the country's economy was to worsen in 1928 and, by that test, which Baldwin himself had chosen in 1922, the government had no economic policy to offer to the electors.

4

I do not think, indeed, that this was the chief cause of its defeat; but that brings me to another part of my retrospect which cannot be written in terms of Baldwin himself. The truth is that, in the eyes of the electorate, and also I think in the eyes of the future historian, the government's chief failure in 1924–9 was its inability to make terms with the United States; or, in other words, its inability to build on the foundation of the debt settlement which Baldwin himself had laid in 1923. It was as a foundation for future confidential relations that the settlement could alone be justified.

That was, indeed, the only justification for the earlier renunciation of the Japanese alliance. But if so, the record of the government of 1924–9 is the record of a missed opportunity.

I know that this is a prejudiced view and that it will be written off by many readers as hindsight born of secretly nursed frustration; but the fact remains that friendship with the United States was as naturally popular in England as friendship with France was inevitably unpopular. Friendship with France was, rightly as I think, the key-note of Austen Chamberlain's settlement of Europe; but he failed to set it, as he wished to set it, in the framework of co-operation with the United States in promoting world settlement and, failing in this, he had no sufficient policy to set before the electorate in 1929.

As he wished to set it – that is what I meant when I said in Chapter V above that I thought this country had to pay a heavy price for the break-up of Lloyd-George's coalition, but that the price fell due almost immediately, rather than ultimately. The price was to confer on Ramsay Macdonald, in American eyes, the chief claim to be the peace-maker of Europe, in contrast to the very muddled record of both Bonar Law and Baldwin – and above all of Curzon – in 1923 during the long-drawn-out entanglement of the Ruhr crisis. The Labour party might be raw; but it seemed a better tiger-shooting companion in the international jungle than the old Tories. That judgment survived Locarno and when my old pro-French journalist friend, Frank Simonds, wrote his book in 1926 *How Europe made Peace without America*, Macdonald was still the hero of it and Chamberlain played only second fiddle to him. It is difficult for this generation to realize how strong was this prejudice or how completely American opinion was dominated at that time by propaganda on behalf of the Labour party – propaganda conducted, one must add, with extraordinarily little sense of international responsibility. As a trivial instance of this, I remember how, on a visit to America in 1930, my advent was heralded by a bitter syndicated article from the pen of Miss Ellen Wilkinson, describing how I had been the chief agent of Tory policy in the starvation of the children of the unemployed. Small wonder that the Anglo-French naval agreement of 1928, in the matter of cruiser building, was taken by both American and disgruntled English opinion as a sign that Britain definitely preferred to keep in step with France, rather than to make any effort to get into step with the United States.

Not that this was by Chamberlain's choice. His first instinct, when he assumed office in the winter of 1924-5 and found himself faced with a boycott in China directed specifically against British trade, was to offer to co-operate with the United States in the Far East along any lines of policy that the Coolidge Administration might prefer. He thought that these advances were rebuffed; but in fact they were hardly noticed. Five years later, Hoover, who both as Secretary of Commerce and as an "old China hand" was Coolidge's natural adviser in the circumstances, told me that the offer had been unacceptable because Britain was already committed in China to joint action with a whole rag-tag-and-bob-tail of interested European powers. There was, in fact, little or no foundation for this suspicion; but Chamberlain made little or no effort to remove the misunderstanding and was, indeed, hardly conscious of its existence. Here, I am afraid – though this must be little more than guess work – there began to grow up in the Foreign Office a practice which did much to stultify its action over the next decade: the practice of keeping negotiations in London and expecting the ambassadors of foreign powers to convey the full weight of British representations to their governments. The first Lord Malmesbury's warning against this mistake was required reading for all entrants into the Foreign Service as late as my day; but it had largely been forgotten. The practice culminated in Sir John Simon's talks to Grandi in the early days of the Abyssinian crisis which J. H. Thomas, I remember, naïvely regarded as sufficient warning to Mussolini. There was, indeed, some justification for the growth of the practice in dealings with the United States, for diplomacy in Washington had been taking a backseat ever since the advent of President Wilson to the White House; and the British Ambassador at Washington from 1924 to 1930 has confessed that he found Hoover "without exception the most difficult American to know whom I ever met".[1] But the American Ambassador in London was a no better channel of communication and his reports, such as they were, carried even less weight in Washington. The Coolidge administration must bear the chief blame for this missed opportunity: but a missed opportunity it was, and the consequence of it was to be plainly seen in the later failure of Anglo-American co-operation in the Manchuria crisis.

To any who had eyes to see, it was evident even earlier in the breakdown of the Geneva Conference of 1927. In 1921 the limitation of naval armaments had coincided with Britain's abandonment of the Japanese alliance and with the attempt to establish peace in the Pacific on the different basis of the Nine-Power Treaty. In 1927 the only issue of substance was whether the United States should set a standard of naval armaments which would stultify the experiment of 1921 by encouraging a race in naval armaments with Japan. The issue centred in the American desire to increase the number of her heavy cruisers, for which her naval experts did not regard the light cruisers, which had been left unlimited by the Washington Treaty, a satisfactory substitute. It should have been the chief care both of Britain and the United States to see that this issue was not raised in mere terms of tonnage or naval "yardsticks", but in its proper context of securing a peaceful regime in the Far East. In the then mood of the United States, such a negotiation would have been difficult; but Chamberlain cannot be absolved from blame for treating it as impossible.

The Geneva Conference itself is hardly worth writing about. It was a mess. With the exceptions of Cecil, intent on disarmament, and Coolidge, caring only for a budget economy, no one on either side wanted an agreement about cruisers or tonnage although some would have preferred it to a breach: to the naval lobby in Washington, disagreement was a more powerful argument than agreement and Churchill desired only that his country should keep its hands free for the future. Of the later London agreement Stimson, its chief author, has said:

'The American delegation was sent to London to get parity.

[1] *The Theatre of Life*, by Lord Howard of Penrith, 1936.

A more ridiculous goal can hardly be imagined. On every ground the United States should have been happy to see the British Navy just as big and strong as the Britishers' pocket book would permit – except of course as this size might stimulate rival building. That America should have no other important object than a fleet as big as the British was utter nonsense ... No treaty without parity would have received ten votes in the American Senate, so the American Delegation brought back parity. What good it did his country, Stimson was never able to say."[1]

It is not worth while to allot the blame between a government which promotes such a Conference in order to extricate itself from an awkward parliamentary situation and one that accepts the invitation, without hope of a successful issue, because it feels a refusal would be no less awkward. In either case, such a conference marks the bankruptcy of diplomacy.

The bankruptcy was all the worse because the problem was, after all, so simple. It is difficult to resist the conclusion that the reaction against Britain of the two Great Powers outside the League of Nations, Russia and the United States, was a reaction, not against any sort of British provocation, but merely against British successful leadership within the League. It was after Britain had most nearly attained leadership of a peaceful Europe at Locarno that her position in China was most directly menaced by a Communist rising fomented by Russia and ignored by the United States;[2] it was after Britain had met that menace by the

---

[1] *On Active Service in Peace and War*, Harper Press, New York.

[2] As a minor footnote to history, it may be worth stating that these Russian intrigues in China had no connection with the Arcos raid in 1927. The Moscow correspondent of the *Berliner Tageblatt* warned the Soviet authorities at the time that no government could be expected to tolerate such blatantly hostile proceedings as those of Borodin and that they must expect a dangerous reaction from London. He himself regarded the Arcos raid as the fulfilment of his prophecy; but in fact there was no connection. The raid was simply the sort of blunder which a temperamental Home Secretary is always liable to commit on misleading information, and which it is difficult for the Foreign Secretary or the Prime Minister either to veto in advance or to refuse to support afterwards. Whether such a Home Secretary would not be well-advised to purge his mistake by resignation, is a matter of opinion.

expedition to Shanghai that the United States set out to humiliate her at the Geneva Conference. Later, in 1935, it was when Britain seemed to have at last plucked up her courage to mobilize the League against Italy in Abyssinia that the American Congress passed the first of its Neutrality Acts. The fact that the net practical result of all the naval conferences of 1927–31 was to legalize the building of three additional heavy cruisers by the United States, is a sufficient sign of the frivolity of the jealousy which was the main motive of American policy. But this jealousy marked the convergence of two currents of opinion which it was precisely the function of a wise diplomacy of the Bryce type to counteract: the old-fashioned hostility to Britain and the newer prejudice of American liberalism against a British Toryism which it identified too lightly with the reactionary "normalcy" of the Harding and Coolidge administrations so repugnant to it at home. In London, after all, a Tory government was a new phenomenon; there had not been such a government for twenty years and the unfamiliar ideals of "Tory democracy" had to be explained. There was an audience for such explanation, a sceptical but not an unreceptive one. It was probably true, as Hoover told me in 1930, that Macdonald had to visit Washington before Baldwin could have been a welcome guest there; but the truth is a serious reflection upon five years of negligent diplomacy.

Hindsight[1] suggests another comment upon the foreign policy of Baldwin's second administration, though it is perhaps too far-fetched to be stated as a criticism. After the Declaration of 1922 Britain's position in Egypt was precarious, for the reasons I have indicated in Chapter V; and the show of strength which Britain was able to make after the assassination of Sir Lee Stack only masked its fundamental shakiness. Lord Lloyd had a policy to remedy, or mitigate, this, right or wrong;[2] the Foreign Office had none. Or rather, it had no policy but retreat, and it did not see that

---

[1] Hindsight, but not mere wisdom after the event. This passage was written some months before the Suez crisis of the summer and autumn of 1956.

[2] His policy may be described as forcing Egypt to 'work her passage' under the Declaration of 1922, undisturbed by premature efforts to regulate Anglo-Egyptian relations by an agreed treaty.

retreat would leave a vacuum which must be filled. Egypt, occupied by British troops or unoccupied, advised or not by British officials, was a country subject, in the language of international law, to a "servitude": the servitude of the Suez Canal. Its trustee-ship for the free navigation of the Canal must one day be rewritten into international law, conformably to the new system of the League of Nations. It is noticeable that even when the treaty of alliance with Egypt, which Austen Chamberlain had so long vainly sought to achieve, was concluded in 1936 after the Abyssinian crisis, the control of the Canal was still left undefined. That was deliberate; for the policy of the Foreign Office was to treat the freedom of the Canal as settled, and *stare decisis*. But it was vain to expect an independent Egypt to confine herself willingly within the all too ambiguous limits of the Constantinople Convention, as they had defined the circumstances under which she might restrict the free use of the Canal in time of war; it was ludicrous to exclude the closure of the Canal from the list of sanctions which the League was authorized to impose on an aggressor. Such a policy could be justified only on the assumptions that Britain's position in Egypt was secure and that she intended to use her power there to control the Canal in the interests of peace; yet Chamberlain's whole policy of gradual retreat denied those assumptions. To amend the Canal Convention with the consent of the United States would have been a ticklish negotiation, but not one beyond the reach of an active diplomacy and, unlike our actual business with the United States, it would have been a negotiation about realities. It is difficult to resist the conclusion that the real reason for not undertaking the negotiation was a desire to retain for ourselves a free hand in Egypt which we had no intention of using freely.

It is impossible to resist here a reference to the nemesis which has overtaken this country's Middle Eastern policy since these words were written. Having found that a military occupation of the Canal Zone bore no convincing relation to the maintenance of the free navigation of the Canal, we withdrew our troops, but went out of our way at the same time, to recognize the "sovereignty" of Egypt over the Canal, as if we expected a rising nationalist movement to interpret that ambiguous word in the light of agreements and understandings which rendered it almost meaningless. We relied, for ensuring the freedom of the Canal, rather on our own right of re-entry than on any international guarantee, only to find that our right of re-entry, when we tried to enforce it, was judged by other nations to be incompatible with the general system of the United Nations. We had renounced our "colonial" responsibilities in Egypt, in so far as we had ever tried to exercise them, more than a generation earlier, only to find that our re-occupation of the Canal Zone appeared to our American friends as (ironically enough) an exhibition of "colonialism". We are now left to substitute, in the most unfavourable circumstances, an international guarantee for our own trusteeship of the Canal, to which we had clung so dumbly for so many short-sighted years.

CHAPTER IX

Crillon, 1929-37

I have stolen this chapter-title from the quip of an American journalist friend in 1915. It was, he said, wholly appropriate that Americans should have fixed their neutral headquarters in Europe at the Hotel Crillon in Paris, for, after all, history records only two things about Crillon. One is Henry of Navarre's message to him from Dieppe: *Pends-toi, brave Crillon; nous avons vaincu à Arques, et tu n'étais pas là*; the other is the picture of him in church on Good Friday, listening to the Gospel story of the Crucifixion, when he was heard to mutter, beating his breast: *Où étais-tu, Crillon?* In other words history only records of Crillon that he wasn't there; and that is all that history would be able to record of the United States in the crisis of Europe. As it turned out, the quip was unfair when it was spoken, though I often had occasion to remember it between the wars. But it would have been a perfectly fair comment on my own political life between 1929 and 1937.

When in the latter year I quitted politics for university administration, I had been largely "out of things" for eight years, between the ages of forty-two and fifty. My position on the fringes of parliamentary life during those eight years does not entitle me to comment much on the conduct of government. Still, I did a little and I watched a great deal; and some of my memories and thoughts may be of service as footnotes to history.

I

The first thing that happened to me in 1929 was, so to speak, something that did not happen. Sometime before the election, Baldwin had sent for me (Chamberlain being away ill) and asked my advice on the choice of a successor to Howard as ambassador at Washington. I confessed myself at a loss, but said I sometimes wondered whether it was not my duty to offer myself. A little later he sent for me again and told me that everyone concerned seemed to agree that I was the best choice, and would I go when the time came for Howard to retire in a few months time? I accepted – and then heard no more about it for nearly three years. Not that I expected to; the appointment was obviously an impossible one for a Labour government to make. Unfortunately, the incident had consequences beyond my personal sense of lost opportunity. The only alternative appointment was Sir Ronald Lindsay. No one could have filled the post better than he; but he was even more needed as Permanent Secretary at the Foreign Office and, in his absence at Washington, the decline in the Foreign Office, I think, began.

Here arises a consideration which both contemporary critics and historians are too apt to overlook. In a civil service government, good or bad administration depends on the maintenance in each government department of a certain *moral*, derived partly from a clear policy dictated by its Cabinet Minister, and partly from an example of steadiness and breadth of view set by its service chief. The history of Foreign Office *moral* after the first war is an unfortunate one. The Office had been trained throughout nearly four years of blockade in a tradition of sympathetic co-operation with the responsible managers of overseas trade, British and foreign. Its members had found in this blockade work a more satisfying field of activity and a more tangible touch with realities and personalities than had been afforded by the political moves and counter-moves of an older diplomacy; and they wished ardently to keep their place in this field. As early as 1916 a Foreign Office Committee, of which I was secretary, had recommended that the Office should retain responsibility for overseas trade after the war, as an essential element in international relations. This report aroused the frenzied opposition of the Board of Trade in the latter days of Runciman's presidency and, out of the Cabinet tussle that ensued between him and a somewhat bewildered Grey, emerged that curious "mixed infant", the Department of Overseas Trade. Though no one fully realized it at the time, this was to some extent a conflict between new ideas of "managed" trade and the *laissez-faire* traditions of the Board of Trade. After the war, the controversy meant nothing either to Curzon or Hardinge, masters of the older school of diplomacy; and the evident tendency of the Office to drift back to the habit of policy-mongering had a good deal to do with the resignation from it of some of my generation.

This is not to say that we were necessarily right. Foreign policy can rarely be defined in terms of tangible national interests; it has usually to deal with too many irrational fishers in troubled waters; and it is at least arguable that, in dealing both with France and Germany in the 'thirties, British foreign policy would have been sounder if it had been less reasonable, less inspired by considerations of economic good sense. But if such considerations must often be dismissed, they can never be ignored; a diplomatist must not be taught to think that they are not his business. Unfortunately that was very nearly the attitude of the Treasury in dealing with the Foreign Office, from the day in August 1929 when Snowden told Henderson that he might just as well leave the Hague Conference and go home, until the weekend in February 1938 when Neville Chamberlain jostled Eden into resignation. Still more unfortunately, the Foreign Office never understood that attitude. They identified it with the quite different issues of the control over diplomatic appointments claimed by Sir Warren Fisher as "head of the Civil Service" and his censorship of Foreign Office papers circulated to the Cabinet on matters involving financial policy. Whatever had been the fate of the recommendations of the 1916 committee, the Treasury was a more formidable rival than the Board of Trade. Neither the Treasury nor the Prime Minister between the wars could have given the Foreign Office a free hand in the economic affairs of a family of nations dominated by the tangled problems of debts, reparations and the gold standard; but a wisely led Foreign Office might have come to a reasonable understanding with them, at least in the five years between 1932 and 1937. As it was, the Office, feeling itself excluded from all deliberations of substance, tended to translate all issues into the romantic terms of a duel between France and Germany – a simple dichotomy which fitted well enough the situation created by Hitler's retirement from the League in October 1933, but not the abandonment of reparations at the Lausanne Conference in June 1932, and afforded no basis at all for an active policy in the Far East, or for the restraint of Italian ambitions in Abyssinia, or for reasonable relations with the United States. From this point of view, Lindsay's relegation to Washington was, I think, almost as much a disaster as Austen Chamberlain's later decision in 1931 not to return to the Foreign Secretaryship.

2

My next unfinished venture in 1929 was the formation of a research department for the Conservative party. I did this at Baldwin's rather half-hearted request as a preliminary job of survey and organization, on the understanding that the department would be taken over by Neville Chamberlain on his return from abroad. On his return, I left almost immediately on a visit to Canada and the United States and, when I came back, he gave me clearly to understand that he did not want me to have any more to do with it. My impression is that we approached the project from two diametrically opposite points of view. He wanted a group of men who would "devil" for him personally, or would at least work out the application of measures which would be given them as the party's policy, and this, at the time, meant mainly the elaboration of a protective tariff; my conception was the more academic one of a group ranging more at large over the whole field of unsolved problems, and suggesting conclusions out of which a party policy might be constructed. Hence his comment to me when he took over, that the leaders of the party did not seem to know what I was after, to which I felt inclined to reply that, after two or three months preliminary work, I hardly yet knew what I was after myself, except that I had convinced myself, at least provisionally, that the problem of unemployment insurance finance was soluble and that the protection of the home market was as essential to the restoration of the steel industry as it was useless as a basis for any system of imperial preference.

As I compare our two attitudes now in the light of after events, I have no doubt that mine was too academic and took too little account of the need for an immediate party programme which might restore the badly damaged *moral* of the party, as it struggled to recover from the blunder of "safety first". On the other hand, such a programme turned out to be unnecessary in the election of 1931, whereas the party suffered much from the absence of a programme of a different kind in the years between 1931 and 1936. In 1931 (whatever the history books may say) the issue of Protection was merged in a general appeal to the electorate to sink old prejudices, as well as personal interests, in a single-minded resolve to restore the economic security of the nation – the old message of "safety first", but with a very different accent; while in 1932 it can hardly be denied that the search for a system of Imperial Preference landed the party in something very like a blind alley. By contrast, in the period 1931–6 and even longer, the party was to feel desperately the need for a domestic policy (quite apart from the issues of foreign policy and rearmament) which might have saved it from the quagmire of amateurish slumming in the "depressed areas" in which I had already been floundering as early as 1928–9. There can never be a final answer to this old dilemma of timing in politics – the dilemma between planning ahead and trimming one's sails to catch the wind of contemporary opinion and contemporary dangers; but it is, after all, the dilemma between research and party management, and it still seems to me to have been a mistake to confuse the two.

The mistake, I think, did not really come home to roost for almost fifteen years. When a committee of the Cabinet was preparing the election programme of 1929, I remember expressing my feeling that "social reform", the idealism out of which Disraeli and Joseph Chamberlain had constructed a new "Conservative" philosophy, was fast becoming worked out as a source of practical policy. One could not, I felt, indefinitely profess devotion to a "free economy" whose unimpeded effect upon the

lives of the people at large needed such continual correction by
State intervention. Nor could I feel that such modifications in a
free economy as could be looked for in this island from the introduction of any sort of "managed economy", Keynesian, protec-
tionist or socialist, would be sufficient to resolve this fundamental
dilemma.

In one respect, at least, these doubts missed the point. This
country was to emerge from the second world war with a social
reform programme which aroused a degree of popular enthusiasm
out of all relation, it seemed to me then, with its real merits. The
"Beveridge Plan" seemed to sweep the country off its feet. Yet
Beveridge's report was, in the main, no more than a sober
arithmetical calculation of the possibilities of a policy which had
long been a commonplace of thought among social reformers, not
least Conservative. It was a striking example of the kind, perhaps
the only kind, of originality within the reach of a political research
orgainization which does not allow itself to be limited too closely
by the expediencies of the moment – and such originality is, for
that very reason, beyond the reach of the workaday politician.
A party which postpones its ultimate thinking until it can be done
semi-publicly for it by an independent commissioner, with the
whole machinery of the civil service at his disposal, cannot complain if its leaders are unready to stand the full blast of this commissioner's conclusions, delivered publicly and without warning.
That still seems to me to be the price that the Conservative party
had ultimately to pay for the misuse of its research organization in
1930 and the following years.

I do not, of course, claim that the Conservative Research
Department could, under any management, have produced anything like the Beveridge Plan in those years. It was, indeed,
obvious enough at that time that a consolidated scheme of social
insurance, together with an extension of health benefit to the
dependents of insured persons, must be the next step in social
reform and, during my suicidal ten months as a "minister without
portfolio" in 1935–6, I did fiddle about a little with such a scheme,
combined with family allowances, on more ambitious, but less

practical, lines than Beveridge's proposals. But I had to do my fiddling privately, out of sight of Neville Chamberlain's mistrustful eye; and, apart altogether from the prospect of war, I could not detach my mind in those months from the overmastering pre-occupation with unemployment sufficiently to contemplate with any comfort a scheme mainly financed out of large insurance contributions which must constitute a direct tax on employment; while it was already plain that any Exchequer subvention to such a scheme had been dangerously mortgaged in 1925 to the finance of contributory old age pensions at the age of sixty-five. During those suicidal months, it was, indeed, the population problem, rather than health or even unemployment, which most occupied my attention and I went so far as to work this out, with much kindly academic advice, in a memorandum which I suppose is still pigeon-holed, *faute de mieux*, in the files of the Ministry of Health; but that problem was even farther beyond the reach of the workaday politician than social insurance. It had, indeed, much to do with the nation's war potential, but its potential for a war twenty years' hence; and I could not induce even Baldwin's middle-sightedness to take any interest in it.

In thus prolonging the tale of my political "reasearch" up to 1936, I am, of course, inviting an obvious criticism. One hundred and thirty years earlier, a few months before Trafalgar, Collingwood had written from his blockading squadron before Cadiz: "The French Government never aim at little things while great objects are in view." That truth is one that British Governments seldom realize until their enemies' designs are almost complete, and they cannot always expect to find a Nelson to save them in the hour of crisis. Looking back from 1956, it may well be asked what I was doing with population and social insurance at a time, two years after Hitler had left the League of Nations, when the future of the British Empire depended wholly on the pace and quality of its rearmament. I can, no doubt, plead in reply that the two preoccupations were not mutually exclusive, and that the Conservative party's amateurishness in dealing with unemployment did not make it more efficient in handling rearmament;

but, at this distance of time, I hardly wish to defend myself against the charge that, during the eight years when I was excluded from administrative office, my state of mind was hardly the stuff out of which political leadership is made.

3

But I should not admit the same charge of fiddling while Rome was burning if it were brought against my main concern during these frustrated years: the preparation of a scheme of federal self-government for India. True, even that project turned out to be more a research study than an experiment in statecraft, for, though it reached the statute-book, the statute was never fully implemented. In a sense, the whole story is one of tragic waste. Churchill complained, and is still complaining, that "the report of the Simon Commission was ignored and no opportunity of debating it was given to Parliament";[1] and on that issue he resigned his membership of Baldwin's "Shadow Cabinet". Yet, in fact, the only part of the Act of 1935 to be brought into force before the outbreak of war was a plan of provincial autonomy closely modelled upon the recommendations of the Simon Report. To that extent, the whole fight was a sham; and, in so far as it was a real fight, each of the contestants was on the wrong side. The only chance of bringing India into the war of 1939, in at least the same sort of temper as she had entered the war of 1914, was to provide her with a representative central government which could make the declaration of war a constitutional act instead of a mere stroke of power; the non-existence of such a government in 1939 wrecked provincial autonomy more fatally than it wrecked the full scheme of the Act of 1935. It ought to have been Churchill who, foreseeing the catastrophe to come, should have pressed for the full scheme; it ought to have been Baldwin, with eyes supposed to be wilfully closed to that catastrophe, who should have taken the easier course of implementing the Simon Report, disregarding the remoter issue of federation. If statesmanship goes by

[1] *The Gathering Storm*, p. 79.

instinct, there is no doubt where, in this matter at least, the right instinct lay in these years.

But in truth statesmanship lies in something more: in a combination between instinct and a grasp of the technical factors involved in a problem. That was Hitler's strength from the beginning of the armaments race; it was, I think, also de Gaulle's strength if he had ever found a sufficient field for its exercise. In England, Ministers have for generations been so accustomed to rely for technical knowledge on the Crown Services, civil and military, that this combination is seldom to be found in one person. This makes for a dangerous weakness in English parliamentary oppositions; for a political leader who has been used to command expert opinion while in office feels lost when in opposition he has to manufacture it for himself, however capable he may be of appreciating technical issues and however wide his past experience may have been. It was, I think, for this reason that Churchill's opposition to government policy in India so failed to carry conviction, in spite of his parliamentary gifts. Certainly, he felt this loneliness himself and he was genuinely hurt when, in a debate in 1932, I jestingly advised the House of Commons to "let his legions thunder past and turn to thought again". He felt himself to be fighting a lonely battle, not only against a parliamentary majority, but also against the formidable array of ministerial and expert knowledge which a government has always at its command; and though I was on the other side, I could not help feeling myself that there was something unfair in the contest. But to play a part in such a combination exactly suited my bent, and I enjoyed the contest more than any other episode of my parliamentary life.

My own introduction to the Indian problem, in which I had taken no previous interest, was unexpected enough. In December 1931, Hoare offered me the Chairmanship of the "Round Table" Committee on Federal Finance, which was to examine the problem in India. After the election of that year, I had been, of course, disappointed not to be offered any place in the "national" government; but I made up my mind almost at once that the one thing a disappointed ex-Minister must not do in the circumstances of the time was to "rock the boat". I was unashamedly Baldwin's man – too much so, some onlookers thought at the time, to have much future of my own; I remember him apologizing for having to leave me out and referring rather vaguely to the Embassy at Washington; and I remember also (though I think on a later occasion) writing him a letter saying that I hoped my tombstone would at least deserve the epitaph: "he did not grumble". I doubt, therefore, whether there could have been much in Geoffrey Dawson's suggestion to me, when he saw the members of the three "Round Table" Committees off at Victoria Station, that Baldwin was wise in giving his disappointed discards something to do abroad lest they make trouble at home. None of this boat load of emissaries was likely to be politically dangerous!

Whether any of us was politically useful, it is not for me to say. Later, I was hurt that I was not included in, or consulted at, the third "Round Table" Conference, and that the Conference appeared to ignore my Committee's recommendations. I concluded that this was to be another of my unfinished beginnings and I was surprised when I was invited in 1933 to be a member of the Joint Select Committee appointed to prepare a final report on the whole problem. This and the parliamentary debates which followed occupied me for the next two years. I wrote almost the whole of the introductory chapter of the Report and some passages in the later chapters, and in the debates I felt myself at home as never before or since in the House of Commons. For that moment, at any rate, Crillon *was* there.

At least, he was there in the only guise which was, perhaps, within his political scope: as a parliamentary technician translating a model constitution of the "unwritten" British type so far as possible into cold print, and adjusting it to the needs of a federated sub-continent and to the cross currents of two cantankerous bodies of opinion in India and at home, with a good enough memory and a good enough eye for argument to make him an effective parliamentary debater. That job still seems to me to have been supremely worth doing, but whether it might have been better done it is still too early to judge.

Certainly, I learnt very little about India from my one short visit there. It was, indeed, very short and, except for one weekend in Lucknow, I did not move from Delhi. My task was the very restricted one of ascertaining whether federation was financially feasible and I decided to take that modest fence at a gallop, for I found on arrival that the "Round Table" Committees were widely regarded by Indian opinion as a move in the delaying tactics which the new British Government was supposed to have adopted. That suspicion was untrue, but if I had worked less quickly it might have seemed to be confirmed in a minority report by at least one Indian member of the Committee. For the answer to the question set us was that federation was just, but barely, feasible; and that answer did not please either the trigger-happy revolutionaries of the Congress party nor the more timid members of the Chamber of Princes who had rashly played with the idea of federation, but were not prepared to face its implications – least of all, perhaps, its financial implications.

This experience raised a doubt which remained with me until the end; whether we, the authors of the new Indian constitution, were wise in making ourselves so completely the prisoners of the Princes. Among the least of these, the glorified feudal landowners of small states, there were some, particularly one, whom I specially liked, and some of the greater had prime ministers, usually trained in the all-India or the Provincial Services, who were qualified to be leading statesmen, if their masters had allowed it; but only one of them was himself a statesman of large views, and he could not alone be strong enough to drag the dead-weight of his colleagues after him. Yet, under the Act of 1935 these men held the keys of Indian constitutional unity; their accession could bring it about; their failure to accede would frustrate it. This was always the one real argument against the federal scheme. It was difficult to devise any alternative way to federation; but this way was rendered more doubtful and difficult by Conservatives in England who insisted that the British Government should "bring no pressure" to bear on the Princes to accede. This always seemed to me to be disastrously short-sighted; the last service that the British Government could have rendered to these its ancient allies was to induce them to face the inexorable alternatives of the future. In the event, as we now know, they chose the alternative of inaction which led inevitably to extinction.

My other doubt about the federal scheme is bound up with the fatal word "Pakistan". That word was never mentioned in the deliberations of the Joint Select Committee; privately, the Indian delegates, not least the Moslems, dismissed it as the rather disreputable dream of a single agitator, called Jinnah. It is, I suppose, doubtful whether the dream would, in fact, have come true had it not been for, first, Hindu arrogance in the days of provincial autonomy after 1937 and, later, the prospect of complete British withdrawal after the war. But, even before 1935, it was something more than a dream; I saw enough of Indian opinion in 1932 to be aware of the attraction exerted upon some Moslem minds by the memory of Sir Edward Carson and by the analogy of Ulster. In the north-western and north-eastern extremities of India, though in no other part of the sub-continent, the nightmare of what Churchill was fond of calling the "blood-bath", which would follow Indian self-government, was to become a waking horror. Could a wiser statesmanship, in 1935 and earlier, have done anything to avert that horror?

I do not know. I was personally not impressed by any of the expedients suggested, then and later, for mitigating Moslem numerical inferiority at the Centre, partly by interposing some kind of regional authority between the Centre and the Provinces and partly by devising a relatively non-political form of executive at the Centre on the Swiss model. The latter was, in 1933–4, the most popular expedient, and I remember exasperating Austen Chamberlain, as the leader of a group in the Joint Selection Committee, by what he thought was my factious opposition to it. The trouble about the Swiss model, I always felt, was that it was the one successful version of an elsewhere uniformly unsuccessful and rather dangerous constitutional invention: the placing of executive power in the hands of a "bureau" of the legislature. That had been the characteristic revolutionary invention of the men of

1789 in France and had been handed down to the Soviet State one hundred and thirty years later. Oddly enough, something very like it is the pattern of English municipal government. Where the non-political convention is observed, it can work excellently, if rather conservatively; where it is not observed, as it usually cannot be in the policies of a Great Power, this form of executive can become either the plaything of irresponsible parties or the ideal instrument of government by a single-party caucus. The exceptional Swiss version of the pattern is even harder to reproduce in a written constitution than the conventions of English parliamentary government; and if Indian politicians could not be trusted with the second, which were after all, familiar to them, there was even less reason to suppose that they could be trusted with the first, of which they had no experience.

In all this I may have been wrong. Perhaps my views may have owed too much to the rather defeatist feeling that, after all, in any peaceful devolution of power, Britain could confer on the nations of her Commonwealth no other form of self-government than that which she had created for herself and had become skilled in practising. A more imaginative statesmanship might not have stopped short at the ineffective expedient of communal electoral lists, but might have ventured on more drastic and more effective safeguards against communal tension. As I say, I do not know. I can only report, as a matter of history, that, in the middle 'thirties, the parliamentary opposition in England to any scheme of Indian self-government at the Centre did not encourage originality of this kind in reformers, for it was the principle of any form of central government other than British that was challenged, and this fundamental challenge pinned the reformers too much to the defensive.

Still, with all these reservations, I think this Report of the India Joint Select Committee may occupy a special place in history. As, a century before, the Durham Report had marked, though remotely perhaps, the origin of the second British Empire; so our Report may come to be recognized, even if as remotely, as the legacy of that Empire to a British Commonwealth of free Nations.

Even if it betrays the weaknesses of the British political tradition, it conveys also its strength – and I cannot but be glad that I had a hand in it.

4

My short interlude as a Cabinet Minister in 1935–6 must be left for separate treatment, covering as it did, in no more than ten disastrous months, both the Abyssinian and the Rhineland fiascos. But I may add here a note upon Crillon's last days in 1936–7, when I worked as Chairman of the British Council.

Here, again, there was, at first sight, some discrepancy between my activities and the times in which I was living. It was the short breathing-space between the occupation of the Rhineland and the invasion of Austria, the first year of the Spanish Civil War and of our own oddly muddled effort at rearmament. What, it might well be asked, were the members of our Foreign Office doing, with the coming clash of arms already in their ears, playing with the neglected idea of "cultural relations"; why should they choose this moment, of all others, to import an ex-Minister to sponsor an agency for introducing European and West Asiatic nations to British music and ballet, British university education, British books, British traditional ideas and the English language?

And yet, I am not sure. Certainly the young men who, in the Foreign Office, were keen on the idea, and had been responsible for launching it, were not "appeasers" and my chief coadjutor and successor in the Council, was, of all people, Lord Lloyd. The truth was that, in the circumstances of the time, if one could do little, in Sir Stephen Tallents' phrase, to "project" British official policy acceptably to foreign eyes and ears, it was beginning to be possible to "project" the British people. That had hardly been possible before. The nation whom Baldwin, in his own words, had set out to "heal" nearly fifteen years before had been a patch-work of resentments and disappointments; from the point of view of my educational experience, its intellectuals had been in danger of jettisoning the traditional values which had made its schools the envy of the Continent, and had seemed to be taking refuge in the

dim regions of an uncertain psychology. More lately, the bad
fairy godmothers who seemed to preside over the birth of the
"national" government had almost brought back the temper of a
much earlier day, of which Chesterton had written: "Men wore
their own white feather as if it were a plume." That mood had
lasted throughout 1933, from a silly resolution of the Oxford
Union in February to the Fulham by-election in October. But
now things had begun to change. In spite of temperamental
lapses, the process of healing had gone on. The new national
unity so surprisingly revealed in the Silver Jubilee of 1935 had
been shaken out of its carelessness about affairs abroad by the
successive shocks of the Abyssinian and the Rhineland muddles
and, amid the confusions of the Spanish Civil War, it seemed to be
rediscovering its capacity for enthusiasm. "The country is angry",
said a friend of mine in the apparently hopeless days after Dunkirk
in 1940, thinking, not of Colonel Blimp, but of Durham pitmen
and their wives – and that was beginning to be true in 1936. More
valuably, perhaps, the nation was recovering, for the moment,
its typical stability. My work gave me one vision of this quality
which I have never forgotten, when I had a pre-view of the Paris
Exhibition in the summer of 1937. There, when the completion of
the Exhibition buildings was being delayed by a lightning strike
of the French trade unions and when, meanwhile, the finished
Italian and Soviet palaces of propaganda were shrieking crude
bombast at each other across the Seine, while the central area
below the Trocadero was dominated by a sculptured group of
self-conscious Nazi pioneers with over-developed muscles, I
found in the half-built and ill-placed British building one solitary
English foreman carpenter, saw in hand, bowler hat on head and
pipe in mouth, working unconcernedly as if the surrounding
fevers meant nothing to him and, moreover, as if he had plenty of
time. A dangerous vision, perhaps, but a refreshing one!

I do not know how much of this the British Council was able,
by its insignificant efforts, to "project" abroad. Probably very
little. My business was simply to bring the Council out of its
initial obscurity and to win for it a respectable Treasury grant,

which, even so, grew only, for 1937–8, to less than £100,000. Apart from this, my chief concern was with our curious unfitness as a nation to export the education which had been the most significant product of our culture. An English schoolmaster or university professor could teach abroad for more than one year only if he were prepared to gamble with his prospects of future employment at home; and, in addition, the secondary schoolmaster must generally content himself, while abroad, with a smaller salary than he could command in England. Emigrant Englishmen and Scotsmen had filled Argentina with independent schools for their own children, but as a nation we had left them to languish and to fall often below the standards of the local State schools they had despised. In Egypt, our record had been no better and the one positive achievement of the Council that I remember in my day was wholly Lord Lloyd's. He raised £30,000 in the City, for the support of British schools in Egypt, and himself toured the Middle East, mainly with this purpose in mind. For the rest, I can claim no more than that we introduced the work to the public eye and that we started a few projects which were later to bear some fruit.

But perhaps I may venture on two quotations from my personal "propaganda" in the summer of 1937 which betray my own state of mind at the time. One is from a graduation address to the London School of Economics that June. "We are," I said,

> "We are committed to the old ideal of the English university: to make men, rather than to preach opinions. The preacher of opinions may make a Youth Movement or a Communist cell or a new political party, but he cannot make a man. In the significant educational jargon of the day, he can teach men 'co-operative habits of thought'; he can expose them to the contagion of ideas; but he knows nothing, he refuses to know anything, of that intimate alchemy whereby the individual soul converts tested knowledge into personal belief and personal belief into social duty. We have shown in the past that we do know that secret; a distracted world looks to us today to prove that we have not forgotten it."

L

My other quotation is from a lecture in Canada that August, more specifically related to British foreign policy:

"The events of the last two years have hardened our views. They have brought us face to face with a temper in the governments both of Italy and Germany which seems to rule out, for the moment, any effort at accommodation. That temper may have originated in reasonable discontents, but it has left those discontents far behind. Today it has become simply the temper of world revolution. It regards armed conspiracy as the normal means of propagating its political creed: it contemplates war as a desirable form of employment for young men who have no other sufficient outlet for their energies. This fever may pass; but so long as it lasts, its victims are beyond the reach of argument."

If this last quotation was, in some sort, my farewell to politics, I am content to let it stand as such; but I cannot help being glad that I was not called on to make it good, or to go back on it, in the dangers and temptations of the next two years.

CHAPTER X

Complicity in Disaster, 1935-6

I

I must begin this chapter with a personal note about my anomalous membership of Baldwin's third Cabinet in 1935-6, if only because Baldwin's part in the episode has been misunderstood. "How Baldwin must have hated you when he gave you the ignominious job of Minister without portfolio", said a leading Labour Minister to me more than ten years later. That was not true. On this, as on other, occasions, Baldwin did not perhaps think as clearly as he might; but he felt, I think, that he could not decently leave me out and that such a post would, at least, provide me with a respectable waiting-room, pending either the reconstruction of his government after a General Election in the autumn or, alternatively, simultaneous vacancies in the Permanent Secretaryship of the Foreign Office and in the Embassy at Washington which he rather vaguely hoped to bring about. When the possibility of any fundamental reconstruction of the Cabinet dwindled after an unexpectedly successful General Election, he would have liked to dispense with my services and trust me to keep quiet in the House of Commons until the vacancy at Washington materialized, and I should probably have acquiesced in this, if I had had twenty-four hours to think it over – though, as things turned out, I should have found it difficult to keep quiet. As it was, I lingered on for four compromising months, and he greeted my resignation in March with relief, as the correction of what he confessed to have been a "political mistake". At an earlier stage, he would, I think, have liked to use me as a co-ordinator of policy in the depressed areas; but Neville Chamberlain was determined to keep that problem in his own not very imaginative or very knowledgeable hands. That is all I need to say in explanation of my presence in the government. From my own point of view, it was a disastrous mistake; but, though I can take only my share of responsibility for my uncomfortable relations with Chamberlain, I have no one else to blame for the mistake but myself.

Perhaps I ought to add one other personal confession. Earlier, one late evening in the winter of 1934–5 Baldwin sought me out in the lobby of the House of Commons and asked me with some amusement: "What have you been saying to Ramsay? He says you told him that the Government was dead." In fact, Macdonald had dined that night with a small group of younger Conservatives with whom I had been working, and I had said something very like this to him. After that, I pressed Baldwin more than once to form his own government. If he had not been pressed in the same direction by many other more influential people, including Macdonald himself, I should today regret my insistence. It was a mistake, even though a change of government had become essential and even though it was not easy to find an alternative successor to Macdonald. And I ought to have known it was a mistake. True, I was not close enough to Baldwin to realize to what extent his health was failing; I could see only that, compared with Macdonald, he seemed a pattern of vigour; but I knew a crisis with Italy was impending and I had no excuse for forgetting his revealing remark to me on the eve of the General Strike. He ought not to have been asked to sign on for leadership in an international crisis.

What I did not know was that Macdonald, while anxious to give place to Baldwin, was insisting that Baldwin should preserve the exact coalition pattern of the existing Government. He even demurred to my inclusion in the Cabinet because it would slightly disturb the numerical proportions of the coalition. If I had realized this, I should not have thought that such a government would be a sufficient reconstruction, or that its makeshift composition was fair to Baldwin.

Of course, I know that this whole story is open to another,

rather devastating, interpretation. I wanted a Baldwin Government, it might be said, because I counted on office in it. Baldwin, knowing that I had, at length, made some parliamentary reputation over India, was shrewd enough to tempt me into a subordinate office which would give me every opportunity to destroy on the Front Bench any reputation that I had made on the Back Benches. And when I had duly done so, he was quick to drop me, while hoping to keep me reasonably quiet by dangling before me a half-promise of a diplomatic appointment. That sounds quite probable, but it is not true; the historian who adopts it might be well advised to remember a phrase of Ruskin's which Churchill quoted in one of his early journalistic books: "It matters comparatively little whether your judgments are just or unjust, but very much whether they are kind or unkind." Historians are not likely to bother about me; but that dictum should be constantly in the mind of anyone who undertakes to write of Baldwin – not, of course, as a plea in mitigation, but as a guide to character and motives.

But my theme in this chapter has little to do with personalities. I remember once, in an off-the-record speech, defining a Minister without portfolio as one "whose acts are the acts of his colleagues, but whose thoughts are his own". The Abyssinian muddle has been often written about, among others by the chief actor in it; but though, as will be seen, I am far from disclaiming personal responsibility for it, it has never been described from quite this semi-detached point of view. That may, at least, be worth attempting.

2

On strict merits, there was little reason to defend the integrity of Abyssinia. That was true by the standards of pre-1914 "power politics"; and, if anything, it was still more true by the new standard of racial "self-determination". In 1906, Britain, France and Italy had agreed by treaty on their "spheres of interest" in Abyssinia if the Ethiopian empire should break up after Menelik's death; by 1918 the break-up appeared imminent, even if it had not already begun. Among the handbooks prepared in the Foreign Office that year for the Peace Conference, was one written by a historian, not by a diplomatist, suggesting the possible lines of a partition according to the principles of nationality; roughly speaking, it contemplated confining the Ethiopian State to the Amharic plateau and treating the recently conquered Moslem and pagan tribes of the south as the materials of a new State or States, whether colonial or independent. The problem was put aside, at the time, as irrelevant and thorny; but it would probably have been tackled if Italy had shown any sign, at that time or in Mussolini's early days of power, of seeking in a new Somalia, at the expense of Abyssinia, the colonial "compensations" which had been half promised her in 1915.

Oddly enough, however, Mussolini took the exactly opposite line. He pressed for the admission of Abyssinia to the League of Nations in 1923 against the opposition, or at least the reluctance, of the British delegates and he concluded a treaty of friendship with her in 1928. These were the obvious, if short-sighted, preliminaries to a policy of "peaceful penetration", and he confessed privately, though not officially, that his challenge to the League of Nations over Corfu earlier in 1923, had been a mistake which he would not have committed if he had had more experience. There seemed, therefore, at that time no reason to apprehend that he would soon depart from the policy of peaceful penetration in order to pick a quarrel with his protégé which must constitute a new challenge to the League. Five years later, however, he began to plan just such a reversal of policy, tempted perhaps by Japan's success in the very similar circumstances of Manchuria. Meanwhile, the stage had been cleared of the men who might have given him restraining advice behind the scenes: Austen Chamberlain, who had established friendly relations with him, though he hardly trusted him and had no admiration for his methods; and the British Ambassador at Rome, Sir Ronald Graham, who had won considerable influence over him after the manner of the old diplomacy, in which personality counted for so much. Graham had retired at his own wish in 1933 at the age of sixty-three, but he believed for the rest of his life that he could have dissuaded Mussolini had he remained at his post for the next two crucial years.

Dissuasion ought not to have been difficult; but it would have to have been of a kind suited to the full scale of Mussolini's impudence: dissuasion in the manner of the old diplomacy rather than of the new, using the language of expediency rather than of law and morals. Whatever may have been his motives earlier, Mussolini did not now want colonial territory; he wanted war, just as Cavour in 1859 had wanted, not Lombardy, but a war which might build a united Italian nation upon the ruins of the Austrian empire. The appropriate argument against this was that the time was ill-chosen, that it was folly to commit the youth of Italy to a hazardous adventure in Africa on the eve of what might well prove to be Armageddon in Europe. Mussolini's concealed preparations had begun almost at the moment when, in October 1933, Hitler had withdrawn from the Disarmament Conference; they were in full swing the following July when Dollfuss was assassinated and an Italian army had to be massed on the Austrian frontier to check Nazi encroachment, while, simultaneously, Britain was announcing a programme of rearmament, coupled with Baldwin's reminder that Britain's frontier was now on the Rhine. From then until the Stresa Conference in April 1935, the overt policies of Britain, France and Italy were concentrated on the formation of a joint front against Germany. Yet even at Stresa, no word of warning about his "diversionary" activities in Abyssinia appears to have been spoken to Mussolini. True, he was not left entirely without warnings after the Walwal incident of December 1934, but they were of the fumbling kind I have already described in my Chapter VIII – conveyed, not through the British Ambassador in Rome, but through the Italian Ambassador in London.

These were the realities of the situation that confronted the new Cabinet at its first meeting in June 1935. I realize them now, but I doubt whether any member of the Cabinet realized them then, except possibly Macdonald. Certainly I did not. My attention was absorbed by the obvious surface fact that here was another bare-faced challenge to the League, such as we had allowed Japan to get away with less than four years before. It was a "unilateral repudiation of treaties", such as the Stresa Conference had just condemned, with implied reference to Hitler, and that condemnation had been pronounced in the name of the "collective maintenance of peace within the framework of the League of Nations". The Emperor of Abyssinia had referred the dispute to the League, with faultless adherence to the forms of its constitution. How could we ever mention the name of the League again if we retreated once more before this open threat of violence? In short, my mood in June, which I freely expressed in the Cabinet and to the new French Secretary-General of the League, was not unlike the mood of so many Englishmen in the following December, when they reacted so violently against the Hoare-Laval agreement.

I think now that I was wrong, but I cannot remember that anyone then, in the Cabinet or outside it, suggested any feasible alternative. A few wished, from the outset, to stipulate that Britain's opposition to Mussolini should stop short of war; but that seemed to me impossible, if it meant that Britain's action should be such as to run no risk of provoking war. If one intervenes to prevent a violent assault on an innocent man, one must be prepared if necessary to knock the assailant down. The other most popular alternative was not to intervene at all, but to confess, both to Mussolini and to the public, as a reason for non-intervention, that we had failed either to give him adequate warning of our opposition until too late or to take the measures necessary to make our warning effective. That might have been possible, if Baldwin's government had been a government of new men, with no responsibility for the negligences of its predecessors. But it was not. Its new members could not even discuss the past frankly with its old members – notably not with the late Foreign Secretary, whose inaction must be the chief item in any confession of past mistakes, and who still sat at the Cabinet table as Home Secretary. And when, a little later, the Cabinet was faced with the unanimous advice of the three Service departments that none of them was ready to incur the risk of war, in view of the depletion of its armaments, there was the same difficulty in expecting the three Defence Ministers and the Chancellor of the Exchequer to display openly the full bareness of the cupboards for which, in a previous administration, they had been themselves at least partly responsible. Never had the disadvantages of a coalition been more clearly demonstrated.

I must not, however, give the impression that the choice was between unsatisfactory, not to say impossible, alternatives and a nobly consistent policy of resistance to aggression. There was very little consistency in the Cabinet's opening move: the despatch of Eden to Rome and the deal he suggested to Mussolini, which was not very different from that contained, six months later, in the Hoare-Laval agreement. If Mussolini wanted war rather than territory, the deal had no chance of acceptance; if our policy was one of correct action by the standards of the League, there could be no justification for pre-judging the issue to be placed before that body. If, moreover, Mussolini was determined to by-pass the League, there could be few less suitable emissaries than the Minister for League of Nations Affairs and the British Ambassador, Lord Perth, who had made his name as Secretary-General of the League. The lead was too obviously one, not from strength, but from weakness and, as such, it could only encourage the aggressor. For these reasons, if for no others, the mission was distasteful to Eden himself, though in the circumstances he could hardly refuse it. I shall have more to say later about Eden's position throughout this whole crisis; but I must say something here about the position of Macdonald.

As I have indicated, I think Macdonald may have been the only member of the Cabinet who appreciated the realities of the situation. He obviously disliked the Eden mission, though he felt the same difficulty in opposing it as small fry like myself felt in criticizing the past action or inaction of our senior colleagues. In spite of my admiration for Austen Chamberlain, I think that Macdonald was the only natural foreign minister of my time, with his Highland sensitiveness to the thoughts and feelings of the foreigners with whom he had to deal. His heart was with the Stresa front, rather than with the League. He had hoped that front would serve to cover his own rearmament policy. For he had such a policy. He had, unfortunately, all the Englishman's inveterate indifference to the Army and he could only fumble with the novel problems of the Air Force; but he ardently desired to rebuild the Navy. It was, of course, one of the tragedies of the years between 1931 and 1937 that neither the Navy nor the Air Force ever lacked either political advocates, wise or unwise, or competent administrators, while the Army was relegated to an obscure corner where its organization was taken for granted. Macdonald's chief complaint against Mussolini's Abyssinian escapade, as he had confessed it frankly at that earlier young men's dinner party where I had been so rude to him, was that it had blocked the chances of a British programme of naval rearmament which might otherwise have been launched with the consent, and indeed encouragement, of all the Powers. He would, therefore, I think, have wished to pursue that policy of realist dissuasion which I have already outlined, rather than to have threatened Mussolini with the legal terrors of the League. His inaction in the months before Stresa, and at that conference itself, can be explained only by deference to his Foreign Secretary and by his own failing health. Whether it was too late to follow this line in June 1935 must remain, it seems to me, the chief doubt about the wisdom of the foreign policy we then adopted.

As I have said that no feasible alternative to that policy was suggested, I ought to mention one authoritative alternative which belongs to a slightly later date, when the form of League sanctions was under discussion. That was Lloyd George's proposal that the Suez Canal should be closed against Italian ships, and against all ships in the service of Italy. That would have been the only effective sanction and it would probably not have been difficult to adopt it with the consent and support of Egypt. It would, however, have been (to say the least of it) an incorrect proceeding, difficult to justify in terms of international law. We should have been using in a "League" war a weapon which we had refused to use even in the war of 1914–18. The League was, in fact, an inadequate "framework" for collective security because, as the Disarmament Conference had sufficiently shown, it could frame only the dead scriptures of Versailles; within that framework there could be neither life nor change, and the only virtue that could fit into it was a correct adherence, in the language of seventeenth century Scotland, to "the law and the covenant". And, as I have already indicated in Chapter VIII, we had failed to make any attempt to write the control of the Canal into the law of the League. In the months that followed I was fond of telling political audiences that supporters of the League must not mistake themselves for a cowboy Vigilance Committee; but I now realize that the Stresa Conference, in spite of its formal invocation of the League, had re-introduced the era of Vigilance Committees, and that the League could not be successfully revived until the dictators had been more strongly challenged than was possible under League procedures. I am left to regret today that we were not lawless enough to adopt Lloyd George's proposal, to break the law with the approval of all members of the League except Italy, and to mend the breakage at our leisure.

The weakness of the League as a league, in the old American phrase, to *enforce peace* was, no doubt, due partly to its idealization by, if one may be allowed the phrase, the "goody-good", culminating in the Peace Pledge ballot where the League seemed to be dragged in as an innocuous postscript to a pacifist declaration. But it was due even more to the League's original constitution. It had been devised to ensure delay before an unforeseen dispute could burst into an unintended war, and its standard sanction of economic boycott was the slowest-acting of all possible war measures. But, as we had learnt to our cost in Manchuria, and as we were to learn again both in Abyssinia and the Rhineland, the characteristic weapon of dictators bent on deliberate aggression is the *coup de main*, and in that context delay and discussion, and even economic sanctions, made no sense at all.

3

Whether this estimate of the situation in June 1935 be sound or not, we committed ourselves in the following months to action within the strict terms of the League Covenant, in so far as those terms were effectively applicable in a League which did not include the United States. Not only did we not close the Suez Canal, but we did not even seek directly to prohibit imports into Italy, because that would involve the declaration of a blockade. In particular, until the very eve of the Hoare-Laval agreement, we did not seek to prohibit her imports of petrol. Such a prohibition, though it could not have been enforced against American or American-controlled supplies, would have been, next to the closure of the Canal, the most effective sanction available to us. Instead, we confined ourselves deliberately to the only sanction which could be applied generally by all members of the League: the withdrawal from Italy of her means of payment for imports. This modified form of boycott should not be written off as obviously ineffective. It was not mere bluff. I think it would be true to say that it would have prevented Mussolini from prolonging his war beyond a single campaign; and neither his own nor other military experts expected that a single campaign would be sufficient. Indeed, he did not want it to be sufficient; like Cavour in 1859, he hoped for a long war. The real objection to this apparatus of half-measures was, not so much that it was an inadequate response to Mussolini's challenge, as that it was an inadequate expression of the public opinion which we exerted ourselves to mobilize.

I have referred rather disparagingly in Chapter III to the American belief in moral reprobation as an instrument of foreign policy. But, indeed, the same sort of criticism might be levelled, as it turned out, against the tendencies of the League of Nations; and the Suez crisis of 1956 has, quite recently, reminded us that in this matter a double portion of the spirit of the League has descended disastrously upon the United Nations. One does not secure unanimous action in important matters by fifty or more governments, large and small, each more or less responsive to its own public opinion, except by the methods of public emotional appeal, familiar to "democratic" nations in their general elections at home. Such appeals have a way of magnifying issues and colouring them by the use of moral language picturesque enough to attract votes. In the years between 1920 and 1935 the temptation thus to overplay one's hand at Geneva had developed in proportion to the unexpected growth in prestige of the Assembly of the League. Crucial issues had tended increasingly to be discussed, not privately in unadvertised meetings of a Council of Great Powers, but with deliberate publicity in the sessions of a semi-parliamentary body; and we had come to congratulate ourselves on what we considered this natural and healthy supersession of "secret diplomacy" by parliamentary methods. We had forgotten that such methods are tolerable in domestic affairs only if their sound and fury are modified by a general tacit understanding that majorities will not in fact, go to extremes, and if the avoidance of extremes is entrusted to a Cabinet working, not only in secret, but under a vow of secrecy. The Council had gone some way towards establishing this sort of understanding in the Chamberlain-Briand era before 1929; but since then the Council's prestige had waned and it had become natural for Hoare to announce his policy, as he did in his celebrated September speech, to an expectant Assembly with every apparatus of publicity.

To do the League justice, however, the convention of moderation, so to speak, had been pretty well established at Geneva itself. Emotional appeals could be trusted to do no great harm there. But they could do great harm to national public opinions, to whom they were, after all, primarily addressed. The comparatively experienced British electorate was less apt than others to be carried away by such an appeal and Baldwin's Ministers can, generally speaking, plead not guilty to the charge, often and naturally brought against them, of having exploited this particular crisis in order to win votes at their General Election that autumn. But even the British electorate – and, indeed, I think, British Ministers themselves – had no idea of the extent to which, behind the public *façade* of "resistance to unprovoked aggression", the statesmen and diplomatists at Geneva had been concerned, from the beginning, to find means of conciliation with Italy, or of the lengths to which they had already gone, before the Hoare-Laval conversations, in the direction of clothing Italy's claim to a "civilizing mission" in Abyssinia beneath the thin disguise of a League "mandate". In this they were following the British lead given by Eden's conversation with Mussolini in the summer, but they did not follow it reluctantly. None of them looked on Abyssinia as an innocent victim, and none of them wished to carry their quarrel with Italy to extremes.

If little was known about these facts by public opinion in Britain, still less was known in the Dominions or in the United States. It was, I think, the chief tragedy of the Abyssinian muddle that this was probably the last chance of making British foreign policy respectable in the eyes of the British nations overseas. The reasons for this were, indeed, mutually contradictory. Canada had got into the mood of demanding evidence that the government in London was prepared to support the League of Nations, if necessary by arms, for other causes than its own national self-interest and they rated British interests in Abyssinia very low, as indeed they were. South Africans, on the other hand, at any rate those who were inclined to follow Smuts in matters of foreign policy, regarded Italian encroachment in Abyssinia as a threat to a very real British interest: to the integrity of Africa and, in particular, to the freedom of the Suez Canal. And American opinion, after its fashion, was simply carried away by the excitement of "sanctions", and by the idea that, this time at least, the British "governing classes" had not gone soft. The lonely American authors and advocates of the League were delighted, after their long isolation (as one of them said to me at the time) to be told by former critics; "well, you were right after all". There was never a moment in the latter half of 1935 when a knowledge of what was actually happening at Geneva would not have shocked public opinion in all these three countries, as well as in Britain itself.

In fact, there was more than one occasion in these months when

Mussolini seemed to be on the verge of accepting from Geneva a settlement very like the one that he had rejected so summarily when it was put to him by Eden. These signs of yielding, compromised though they were by press leakages, indicated the effectiveness of even the half-sanctions which had been put into operation and Hoare can hardly be blamed for thinking that this double policy of coercion and conciliation might save both the League and the Stresa front from collapse. The policy was, of course politically risky. Churchill might have described it (but did not) in the words he had used on one occasion some years before in speaking of the confusions of government in Dublin soon after the Irish Treaty, as a "duality which verges on duplicity". But the reason why it failed was mainly that British public opinion was not prepared for it; and the reason why public opinion was not prepared for it was, frankly, that Ministers had not clearly envisaged what a reconstruction of north-eastern Africa might involve.

But, to be honest, the policy was risky in another sense and the unpreparedness of public opinion was not the sole cause of its failure. The Cabinet had been warned at the outset that none of the three Services was fit to fight a war in the Mediterranean, without, at any rate, endangering its fitness to fight a war on the Rhine and in the North Sea in the near future. War on the Rhine was in every Minister's mind as, at any rate, a distinct probability, from the moment of the first formation of the Government. Yet the Cabinet had decided to show force in the Mediterranean even though they did not intend to use it there. In these circumstances, they were to some extent playing against time; how long would it be before Germany was ready to challenge them, more seriously, perhaps than Mussolini had the power or the will to do? And, as appeared increasingly with the lapse of time, they were playing from a weak hand. The Mediterranean fleet rode, to say the least, uncomfortably at its anchors in the harbour of Alexandria; it was inadequately equipped to defend itself against the sort of attack which might be made upon it there; but it was still less prepared to venture westward to any roadstead within reach of the Italian air force. Its mere reinforcement by a single battle-cruiser, in the first days of the crisis, had been sufficient to clear the Mediterranean of Italian surface ships; more fully reinforced a little later, as it was, it could no doubt have won a fleet action against the Italian navy; but, so long as the Suez Canal was deliberately left open, it was not likely to be given the chance of such a victory, and it was in no position to break the deadlock. Even more certainly, the deadlock could not be broken on land; the only part which the British Army could be expected to play was to over-insure the safety of Egypt against a highly improbable Italian invasion from the Western Desert. Men who have thus to play a weak hand against time need, at the very least, a reasonably offensive spirit and sound nerves; and, whatever virtues the Baldwin Cabinet may have possessed, it certainly possessed neither of these. Hence the almost unintentional blunder of the so-called Hoare-Laval "pact".

It will be seen from this estimate that, in my view, the importance of that "pact" itself has been much exaggerated. It could reasonably be claimed that the negotiations at Paris were conducted under the authority of the League and *ad referendum* to it. They were not a betrayal of the League; if there was any betrayal, it was the League which betrayed the expectations of its supporters and in that sense, the betrayal had begun long before. The League's sin, committed (be it confessed) on the impulsion of Britain as its leading and most active member, was, not that it had sought a compromise with Mussolini, but that it had misled the public opinion of the world. The whole crisis proved the fundamental weakness of the League; that, though it depended utterly upon the force of public opinion it had no means of guiding public opinion.

Nor do these negotiations need to be justified by complaints of French unco-operativeness in our half-policy of resistance to Mussolini. We had hardly expected – certainly we had not relied on – the active military co-operation of France; nor did we need it in order to establish naval command of the Mediterranean. I did not, therefore, share the exasperation of some of my colleagues, and, I think, of Hoare himself, at the unresponsiveness of France. Speaking for myself, what had impressed me most in Laval's evasions during these months, was how slowly and cumbrously mobilization had come to work under the French military system. Britain, with all her unpreparedness, could mobilize what power she possessed with a tithe of the delay and inconvenience that must be entailed on a French government. That was a significant comment on de Gaulle's book published in the spring of 1934; it was to prove a fatal handicap in the Rhineland crisis of the spring of 1936; but it had, of course, little importance in relation to Abyssinia. Deeply as everyone distrusted Laval; strongly as every British Minister must have resented his shiftiness in having bought a renewal of co-operation with Italy at the price (one could not help suspecting) of promising her a free hand in Abyssinia, without consulting his allies – in spite of all this, might we not, rather, have congratulated ourselves on having this side-door of access to Mussolini for the purpose of the compromise with him which was one half of our policy?

But side-doors are for the use of diplomatists, not Foreign Ministers – especially Ministers in bad health, bound for their holiday and especially side-doors in the purlieus of Parisian politics, habitually red-carpeted with indiscretions. The fatal fault of the Hoare-Laval meeting was that it was badly managed. I need not labour this point; it has long been sufficiently obvious. But I now realize that the bad management was not irretrievable. The Cabinet ought to have accepted the agreement on Hoare's return from Switzerland and defended it in the House of Commons, in spite of the storm which it had aroused in public opinion. Both the House and Mussolini, there is little doubt, would then have accepted it too. The mistake of which I am personally most ashamed is that, at this point, I added my voice to others among Hoare's colleagues in favour of rejection. I have already confessed how unprepared I had been ten years before for the excitability of public opinion, and now I was frankly "rattled" by it. I was always ready to defend the agreement, but not, I felt, as a Minister. Though there was nothing in my own election speeches which I should have needed to unsay, the Government's record was, perhaps, hardly clean enough – or, at any rate, clear enough – for their defence of the agreement on the morrow of the election to

M

carry conviction, so long as they remained in office. So I thought then, but I was wrong. If Abyssinia was betrayed, its betrayal was marked by this rejection of the agreement, rather than by the agreement itself.

I hope I have at least made it clear, in this account of bad management, that I have no wish to slur over mistakes; but, ever since these events, I have been shocked by a tendency among on-lookers to lay responsibility for the Government's mistakes upon Anthony Eden. In my small circle in Northumberland in 1939, it was not Baldwin who seemed to be chiefly blamed for the descent into war, but Eden. It was, no doubt, unfortunate that the exaggeratedly publicized mobilization of the League in 1935 should have been in the hands of the one member of the Government whose personality most easily attracted publicity; but it was doubly unfortunate for him that he was perhaps also the member of the Government who had least sought that task and had the most serious doubts about it. He had had no share, owing to illness, in the curious silences of Stresa; he had positively asked Baldwin not to appoint him to the Foreign Office as a number two to Hoare; he had not liked his mission to Rome and he distrusted the lengths to which Hoare went in his September speech at Geneva. He must, of course, bear his share of responsibility for the policies of the Cabinet of which he was a member; but I know of no more significant instance than this of the danger of attempting to go behind the doctrine of joint responsibility in order to allot personal blame to an individual Minister.

If one is to dream of might-have-beens, I sometimes wonder now whether it might not have been possible for Baldwin to have both persuaded the House of Commons to accept the Hoare-Laval agreement and then have immediately resigned, thus per-mitting a complete reconstruction of the Government under the leadership of Austen Chamberlain. This would have been an unprecedented parliamentary manoeuvre, but not perhaps a wholly impossible one. If it was impracticable, the chief obstacle to it would have been Chamberlain's health. Yet, if one feels that this was the moment for Baldwin to resign a task which he should

never have been pressed to undertake, one has to remember that
the King died within a month of the parliamentary debate on
Abyssinia and that Baldwin's resignation would, as it turned out,
have deprived him of the opportunity to render his last and best
service to the country at the end of 1936.

4

Anyhow, apart from the special problem of the new reign, there
was only one thing for Baldwin's government to do after the
Abyssinian collapse, and that one thing was rearmament. I had got
the impression in the previous June that, in the eyes of permanent
officials at least, that had been from the outset the chief task of the
new government. The Abyssinian crisis had diverted attention
from long-range planning and anything like a large programme of
expenditure must probably await the general election; but now, in
January 1936, the Government's hands were free and they could
take up the task.

They did so, but without, it seemed to me, much sense of
administrative drive. The problem struck me, first and foremost,
as one of administrative speed and I was irked by the academic-
minded insistence of so many critics at that time outside the
Government that we should linger, first of all, over deliberations
about the kind of war for which we proposed to rearm. It reminded me of Uxbridge worrying Wellington for his battle plans
on the morning of Waterloo. Obviously we were preparing, as so
often before in history, for a war in the Low Countries in which
we should not be the attacking party; the defensive which had
been our historic role was now imposed on us by the conditions
of a League war, or something like it, which dictated that we
should conform to the strategy of an aggressor. Within the limits
of that stategy, the best we could hope for was the chance of a
limited tactical offensive. The scope and scale of such an offensive
would depend upon the development of the aggressor's strategy
before the outbreak of war or in its earlier stages. In theory, they
could have been infinitely greater in January 1936 than they were
three years later when the Rhineland and Austria had been occu-

pied and Czecho-Slovakia destroyed – so much greater, indeed, that they might have shifted the main scene of war from the Low Countries to the Danube. But in that case no British Army could hope to play more than a secondary role to the French on the main scene and, even before Hitler's march of unopposed conquest, it had become evident that French military thinking was tied to the defensive. In January 1936, therefore, the best contribution which a British Army could hope to make to a tactical offensive was already a highly mechanized and armoured expeditionary force, with adequate air cover, operating against the right flank of a German attack on the north-eastern frontier of France. Such a force would, moreover, provide that "preventive and repressive weapon of manoeuvre" which de Gaulle had called for in France two years before, to counter any attempt by Hitler to clear the ground of Central Europe of potential enemies in advance of a declaration of war. The creation of such a force was, therefore, the obvious planning target for any rearmament policy, and its creation in the next four years would call for a whole-hearted concentration of administrative energy.

Unfortunately, it was such concentration that was lacking. The prime mistake seems to me to have been the creation of the post of Minister for the Co-ordination of Defence. My name was talked of a little in connection with that appointment, but I did not covet it. It was infected from the start by the craze for speculative planning by civilians of which I have spoken. The central point of danger and of opportunity was the neglected administration of the Army. The damning weakness of the War Office was that, unlike the Admiralty and the Air Ministry, it had never known how to *buy*. At least, its purchasing ability had been limited to the stores and transport of a quartermaster-general. The typical figure of British military history at its best had been Wellington in the Peninsula, faultlessly organizing the supply of food and small arms ammunition to troops in the field, but waiting eternally for the Horse Guards to send him a siege-train. So French had waited for high explosive shells in 1915; so we should find ourselves waiting for tanks in 1940. After the General

Election of 1935 I did covet the War Office, and I still feel that I could have supplied the kind of drive required there, but there were, of course, overwhelming reasons against such an appointment. For one thing, I should not have had the confidence of the Chancellor of the Exchequer; for another, the appointment of a young able-bodied non-combatant could have carried no conviction in the circumstances.

Administrative inadequacy is, indeed, my general diagnosis of this country's unpreparedness in armaments. The old charge against Baldwin that he persisted in lulling the nation into a sense of false security in spite of Churchill's warnings has become more and more difficult to sustain the more the facts are studied. I think that the truest judgment was Lord Lloyd's, expressed to me in retrospect about the time of Baldwin's resignation in 1937: that the country had begun serious rearmament one year too late, but that the government could not fairly be charged with any longer delay than that. The long hunt for some agreed limitation of armaments, which had lasted up to 1934, always seemed to me, indeed, to be a disastrous diversion of effort, but not so much because it delayed British rearmament, as because it approached the main issue of Germany's eventual equality of status in a peacefully organized Europe from the direction which must be most offensive to France. Lloyd George had made that discovery when he had dreamed in 1919 of basing the disarmament of Germany on a general international agreement abolishing conscription. France was tied to the idea of national service as an essential expression of democracy; and later de Gaulle was to struggle vainly to argue that this idea, taken by itself, could give France only a "mass of manoeuvre" too unwieldy for any manoeuvre called for by the conditions of modern warfare. But the blame for this diversion of effort must lie not with those who gave the ill-considered diplomatic assurances to Germany at Versailles, to which Churchill constantly refers in his book, but with those who deliberately committed themselves to Article Eight of the Covenant of the League of Nations. No government in this country could have disentangled itself from that commitment until Germany deserted the Disarmament Conference at the end of 1933, though Macdonald's Government might then have more abruptly terminated what had become little more than a farce. Even as it was, Churchill has argued that this country was not so unprepared eighteen months after Lloyd's verdict, at the time of the Munich crisis, as to have been incapable of a decisive resistance to Hitler's encroachments in Central Europe. But I am afraid that neither Baldwin nor Chamberlain, nor anyone else concerned, can be absolved from the other charge: that, the policy of large scale rearmament once decided, the government fumbled with the task. And the heart of the fumbling was at the War Office.

Whatever the faults of the Admiralty and the Air Ministry, they had always, so to speak, kept themselves in training for re-armament. The weakness of the Admiralty had been, I think, a certain off-handedness in the more scientific sides of planning; their Lordships had rashly disbanded their Corps of Naval Con-structors at the end of the first war, even before they had com-mitted themselves to the naval holiday of the Washington Treaty; and, by the time of the German agreement of 1935, they had naively jumped to the conclusion, on no sufficient scientific advice, that they had taken the measure of the submarine menace. The Air Force were, of course, handicapped by the nature of their equipment; though, like the Admiralty, they knew how to buy, they had to reckon with an even longer gap between order and delivery and a much higher rate of wastage. This had been the one justification for the priority given to "air parity" in the political controversies of the time. But the War Office, with on the whole the easiest task of all, had sunk into a far deeper state of dereliction, especially in the wasted years 1931–5; and the planless-ness of the General Staff had deprived not only the Army itself but also the Air Force of any considered standards of preparedness. I have spoken of a mobile expeditionary force whose task should be a tactical offensive, as the obvious target at the beginning of 1936 but, though this commended itself then both to Neville Chamberlain and to Eden, the mere decision to send an expedi-

tionary force to France at all was never formulated as a policy
until (I take this information from books) the Anglo-French
military conversations of March and April 1939.[1] Meanwhile,
for three long years, the provision of air cover and support for
an expeditionary force could not arise, and the Air Force was
encouraged to conceive its role as essentially defensive. In the
event, it was this conception and not merely shortage of planes
that led the Air Staff to reserve its Spitfires in 1940 for a defensive
Battle of Britain and to leave the British and Allied armies, in the
short campaign before Dunkirk, with little defence against
German dive-bombers and parachutists. It was not until, at long
last, an Army commander came to envisage the practical problems
of a military offensive in the Western Desert that the Tactical Air
Force was really born.

If one is, to any extent, to distribute blame, for all this, the main
responsibility for the long decline in War Office thought and
moral must, no doubt, be borne by its political chiefs; but some
responsibility must, I suspect, be attributed also – not, indeed, to
the Treasury itself – but to the queer infiltration into the War
Office of indirect Treasury control. In most other departments,
the acknowledged dependence of departmental finance officers
upon the Treasury – a far older tradition, be it noted, than the
location of the headship of the Civil Service in the Treasury –
worked, in my experience, tolerably well and did not conflict
with reasonable loyalty to their departmental chiefs; but in the
War Office, by all accounts, long tradition had built up its
civilian finance officers in time of peace into a crippling *imperium
in imperio*, intent upon checking every initiative of the professional
soldiers. It was, I think, on this split personality in the War Office
that the famous "ten-year rule" of 1928 exerted its worst influence,
assuming, as it did, that there would be no major war within ten
years of any given Budget. The rule, so Churchill has said, was
tacitly dropped in March 1932, but Halifax's account[2] of the War

[1] For instance, Mowat, *Between the Wars*, p. 630; Grigg, *Prejudice and Judgment*,
p. 333.

[2] In his *Fulness of Years*.

Office, when he took it over in the summer of 1935, makes one wonder if news of its abrogation had ever percolated to that office during the next three years. Vital as real Treasury control must be to the efficiency of any government, this kind of infiltration is a danger against which any government must be continually on its guard.

5

I have written thus, largely on the strength of impressions gathered during a brief three months' lingering on the fringe of rearmament committees. That interlude ended with my resignation, but not before Baldwin's government had been challenged by Hitler in the Rhineland and had refused the challenge. I took some trouble to detach my resignation from this crisis, in the midst of which it happened to take place. To have linked the two would have been to falsify my reasons for going; but I was, in fact, by no means happy either about the government's handling of the crisis or about its handling of rearmament. My feelings about the second I have already described; I must here touch briefly upon my feelings about the first.

To begin with, the government had sapped its own *moral* for some months past in its tentative thinking about a future settlement with Hitler. Ministers both in London and Paris had got into the habit of treating the neutralization of the Rhineland as expendable for such a purpose. Of course, *moral* had been sapped also by the course of events in Abyssinia and by the feeling that it would be impossible, for some time to come, to reanimate the forces of collective security which had just been so ignominiously routed. But if there was thus no heart in the resistance of governments to Hitler's challenge, there was still less heart in public opinion. This was the only sort of situation where a statesman can ever be justified in pleading that the unreadiness of public opinion has made right action impossible, for here right action had to be decided in a matter of hours and, once the governments concerned had got themselves involved in conversations and explanations, any right action became impossible. Oddly enough, it fell to me to make the first public speech on the morrow of Hitler's invasion, addressing a long-arranged meeting of the League of Nations Union in Birmingham. I could say no more, in advance of any Cabinet decision, than to remind my audience that there was a system of public law in Europe, observance of which must be maintained and, if necessary, enforced; but that platitude, which, I remember, was enough to attract Churchill's approval, was enough also to arouse the opposition of all my hearers from the Roman Catholic archbishop on the platform to the rank and file of trade unionists in the body of the hall. I did not take that opposition too seriously and, a day or two later, I remember joining Duff Cooper in a demur to Baldwin's assumption that public opinion could not be brought to support military action; but the opposition, it must be confessed, was serious enough to give any Prime Minister pause, especially when reinforced by the hesitancies and ambiguities of French policy.

I resigned at this point and I have no direct knowledge of the conversations with the French and German governments which were then still in progress. But perhaps I may add a postscript. Our failure at this time to react immediately to Hitler's challenge was, I think, the worst of all the errors of British governments in the 'thirties – far worse than the superficially more ignominous muddle over Abyssinia. It is probably true, as Neville Henderson said, that this was our last chance of stopping the growth of the German menace without war. If, in Churchill's phrase, the war of 1939 deserves to be called "the Unnecessary War" this failure is the crucial test of its non-necessity, rather than either Churchill's own suggested test of the Allies' failure to stop conscription in Germany, or the test suggested by others of the Allies' failure to make sense of the Disarmament Conference. It was, at any rate, a more easily spot-lighted failure. But, whichever test is adopted, it may be worth while for the future historian to consider whether the failures of successive governments and oppositions in Western Europe and America are sufficiently accounted for by Stimson's outburst in 1932: "We are constantly shut in by the timidity of governments. . . . The time has come when somebody has got to show some guts."[1] I certainly have no reason to pride myself on my physical courage; but I doubt whether physical cowardice was exactly the failing of most of the men whom I knew and worked with in these years.

In this connection, I remember my last meeting with Baldwin in the Cabinet Room of 10 Downing Street, rather less than a year after my resignation and not long before his final retirement. We were not talking politics, but he volunteered the reflection that, in retrospect, he felt that the only thing he had to regret in his record was that he had underrated the lengths to which Hitler would succeed in carrying Germany with him. That may not be far from the truth; the real cause of British backwardness may have been what seemed in English eyes to be the sheer unexpectedness, indeed the incredibility, of Hitler. Plenty of Englishmen feared and distrusted Germany and some thought that they had taken the measure of her General Staff; but many of these latter thought, perhaps rightly, that the General Staff had accepted the idea of a small professional army, as de Gaulle was to do, and had set itself a standard for such an army which, given any reasonable programme of expenditure, would postpone a war of revenge for perhaps a generation. On this assumption there was nothing much wrong with the British Government's policy up to, perhaps, 1934; and Churchill's earlier speeches were, perhaps, discounted because of what seemed a romantic lack of discrimination. Churchill did not himself (so far as I know) quote Bruening's alleged dictum in 1932 that he had lost power *hundert Meter vom Ziel* "within a hundred yards of the winning post"; but many people of Churchill's way of thinking were fond of quoting it, with the implication that the world had nothing to regret if Germany slid down the slippery slope from Bruening to Papen, Schleicher and Hitler. A blitzkrieg had no terrors for men who had already had visions of several tank corps concentrated in the forests of the Palatinate. And in his first year or so of power, Hitler impressed English visitors as little as he had impressed Hindenburg in 1932. Lord Lloyd, for instance, experienced administrator and friend of

[1] Stimson and Bundy, *op. cit.*, p. 281.

Churchill, did not think that he had the makings of a great man and to more sophisticated critics of politics he was still almost a figure of fun. That he would succeed, in little more than five years, not only in mobilizing a nation and abolishing its unemployment, but in equipping a great army and in bringing the dreams of a new strategy within the bounds of reality, seemed to English observers, official and unofficial, wholly incredible.

It is the weakness of Mr. Darcy that he can only despise a cad and laugh at an adventurer, that he has no eye for the exceptional and no sense of the uncanny. Perhaps it is the fault of his education that he has not read the meaner descriptions of the destroyers of mankind, such as Metternich's portrait of Napoleon, and has not learned that they are seldom "great" in his gentleman's understanding of that word. Their historic hall-mark is a different one. I do not know whether I have picked up a phrase about Napoleon from history or only from an historical novel, but it seems to me fatally true: *Il déshonore tout le monde.* In these years before 1939, no public man in England or in France was to escape this spreading dishonour.

CHAPTER XI

Retrospect, 1921-37

Like most old men, the autobiographer is apt to let his mind wander before his end. My story has reached the point when, in 1937, I left politics for university administration; but I am tempted to linger a little over my memories of these sixteen years, picking up bits of litter that I have left unnoticed in my narrative and trying to pull together some of my impressions of men and things.

I

I suppose no actor on the political scene in those years, however minor his role, could leave it without an acute sense of his own inadequacy. To begin with, there was his inadequacy to the hopes of returning soldiers, who felt that they had said "goodbye to all that" and had earned the right to some rather wonderful future. Later, there was his inadequacy to the discovery that the goodbye had been premature, that the immediate future would be rather darker than the past. He could not live up, in the 'twenties, to Curzon's rash peroration in the House of Lords: "The world's great age begins anew: the golden years return"; but neither, in the 'thirties, could he frame convincingly Shelley's final warning which Curzon forgot: that men of good intentions should beware of "draining to its dregs the urn of bitter prophecy", lest they find themselves unable to give any comforting answer to the question, "must hate and death return?" Few of us who had passed through the Paris Conference could meet the first years of peace with any gusto of hope or confidence; still fewer, as their forebodings began to come true, could meet the return of hate and death with any gusto of courage. Gusto, indeed, was what we lacked; the best of us were a low-spirited lot; and our low spirits sapped our capacity for the best kind of political leadership.

The exceptions among us in the 'twenties were, of course, Churchill and Birkenhead and, of the two, Birkenhead always seemed to me potentially the greater man, both in intellect and in mere force of personality. His gusto, even in his most prodigal moments, had always, unlike Churchill's, an adult quality. If this seems an eccentric judgment, it is only, I think, because his extraordinary capacities, mental and physical, turned so completely in the end to tragedy. His story is too sad a one – and too well-known – to linger over; but I always felt that (surprisingly enough, perhaps) he deserved some of the praise once given to Churchill by T. E. Lawrence, when he told me in 1921 that he would rather follow Churchill than Lloyd George, because Churchill had more "essential goodness". That was certainly true of Churchill; his gusto had always a touch of piety in it, the more so the older he grew; his failing was that his gusto was aroused only by issues which he felt to be large enough to deserve it and, if real issues were not large enough, he would use his imagination to exaggerate them. Asquith once said unkindly of his talk that one could see him manoeuvring his subject until he could set it – and himself – in the strongest possible light. I got my first taste of this quality of his in 1914 as I read in the Foreign Office his telegrams from Antwerp, and realized his dangerous, though potentially invaluable, gift for making an ill-timed adventure seem, for the moment, retrievable. A later and more hostile colleague described him to me as that rarest phenomenon among Englishmen, a natural militarist. That was, I think, untrue; but it was true that his imagination was most easily moved by the idea of a display of power. I remember him once sketching to Neville Chamberlain a housing campaign which might touch the imagination of the country, in terms of national organization on the most grandiose scale; and I remember, too, his disappointment at Chamberlain's desire rather to revive the ordinary building industry of the nation, so as to make working-class housing once more one of its normal economic functions, needing no special government activity to stimulate it.

I think this contrast of temper came out in all that followed, until it culminated in Churchill's breach with official conservatism soon after the fall of the second Baldwin administration. In his own words, his "idea was that the Conservative Opposition should ... identify itself with the majesty of Britain", while Baldwin, he guessed "felt that the times were too far gone for any robust assertion of British Imperial greatness".[1] It would obviously be wrong to call either Chamberlain's attitude on housing or Baldwin's on India a low-spirited one; a policy of limited aims may, at worst, be called a pedestrian adherence to facts and, at best, it may have the supreme virtue of generosity; but it is one that conveys too easily to friend and foe the impression of low spirits, and, when confronted with genuine crisis, has a way of degenerating too quickly into a really low-spirited habit of mind.

Perhaps the contrast may be best judged by a remoter example: that of the clash between Hoover and Franklin Roosevelt in the United States. Hoover's work as Secretary of Commerce in the 'twenties has been naturally underrated by Englishmen as a merely materialistic pursuit of "Coolidge prosperity"; but he himself regarded it rather as a demonstration of the potential virtues of a "free economy" and he did come near to achieving something of the political reconciliation which, in another guise, was Baldwin's constant aim. An ardent follower of Theodore Roosevelt in 1912, who prided himself on being a Liberal, told me when we met again in Washington as late as 1930 that Hoover had achieved by mere business administration almost all the aims which had generated the "Bull Moose" enthusiasms of twenty years before. But, in those years of achievement, Hoover had not the art to express, in public speech or action, the essential generosity of his ideals; as one of his Cabinet said of him after he became President, he "was fighting hard in a great battle, but there was no zest anywhere". And in the succeeding economic crisis, though he faced it with courage and never lost confidence in a future revival, he could not compete with Franklin Roosevelt in high spirits and, therefore, in convincing power of leadership. Yet it is arguable that his view was the more nearly right and that, until the war came,

[1] *The Gathering Storm*, p. 44.

Roosevelt, with all his high spirits, accomplished nothing of permanent value; it is even arguable that, in the latter days of war itself, Roosevelt miscalculated profoundly and disastrously all the forces of good and evil which were to dominate the post-war world. All the same, the figures of Roosevelt and Churchill will be long remembered as dominating their times, simply because they were, so to speak, happy men of action. And that we of Baldwin's clan were not.

Of these two figures, Churchill was, to my mind, by far the greater; but unhappily he had not Roosevelt's power of at least appearing to make political sense of economic problems. I have said nothing in my narrative of Britain's return to the gold standard at parity with the dollar in 1925. Churchill has always complained that he was badly advised on this issue; but in fact he had been sufficiently warned beforehand that the decision was a political one, and the charge against him, as against all of us who were then his colleagues, is that he did not appreciate its political implications. I am even now not sure that our decision was wrong in itself; it was certainly a defensible choice for an island so dependent on food and raw material from overseas, and it did in fact do much to raise the standard of nutrition of the worst-paid workers of the country – even, I think, of the unemployed; but, as certainly, we failed to take any political measures which might have made the resulting dislocation of the exporting industries tolerable; and that failure prejudiced the whole future of Baldwin's administration. I remember the managing director of a great engineering firm criticizing our action to me at the time, on the ground that we had not thought to levy a special income tax, to balance, at least in appearance, the relative sacrifices we were imposing on the wage-earner and the *rentier*. That might be a doubtful expedient; but it would have made more political sense than the new scheme of old age pensions with which we did accompany this fateful decision. This was not the sort of issue which ever touched Churchill's imagination, or, if it did touch him in this sensitive spot, he was inclined, perhaps, to think of the gold standard simply in terms of "the majesty of Britain", without calculating how much he might be overstraining that majesty.

Still less, of course, how he might be overstraining his own reputation. One of the results of this heedlessness, perhaps its worst result, was to diminish him in the eyes of many who were then his colleagues. We had all shared the same heedlessness. When the Cabinet finally "voted for gold", I think none of us really knew what we might be doing. But it was Churchill's recommendation and not for that cause alone, but because of all he said and did as Chancellor of the Exchequer during the next four years, I confess that I formed a totally wrong estimate of his practical abilities. The estimate seemed to be confirmed in the next decade by his record over India and the Abdication. I never underrated his speeches on armaments and foreign policy, but I thought, frankly, that, except as an inspired journalist in politics, he was "played out"; and I could not complain now if that crashing miscalculation were judged to be the misunderstanding of a high-spirited man by a low-spirited one. In much the same way, a more experienced observer of the American scene confessed to me that, until their first meeting just after the election of 1932, he had thought Roosevelt to be only a "play-boy". I can at least plead, that having known the man, I never made that mistake and never underrated the value in American politics of one who seemed often to be a Peter Pan, constantly immersed in "awfully big adventures". Distance may or may not lend enchantment to a view, but it certainly lends perspective.

Using "low spirits", as I have done, in a neutral sense without implications of praise or blame, I suppose Baldwin must himself be classed among the low-spirited. But, if so, he made the defect almost a virtue. He had enough natural high spirits to love good company, and he liked it homely and robust, even a little earthy; but he did not find this outlet among politicians. His whole public life was a conscious sacrifice of the way of life he preferred; and he would take his ease at a rare Worcestershire County dinner with a holiday sense of relief. He craved friendship, but his bent was to choose his intimate friends outside politics and as far as possible away from the doubtful obligations of party relationships.

His constant foreboding was that he would lose his political friends on retirement. Great as was my affection for him, I cannot claim to have been at any time intimate with him; but we had what I can only describe as a theoretical liking for each other and he had hoped to see more of me in the loneliness of his last years, which he foresaw. I failed him in that hope, partly owing to circumstances, partly from slackness on my part, and partly because, in my remote North, where I was busily at work, I never realized until too late the extent of his dereliction. That being his temper, he faced his self-imposed task of leadership with fortitude, but never with relish. Low spirits of this type have a dignity of their own; they may be a political fault, but they have, after all, been the characteristic of many "holy and humble men of heart"; and as such many of us will remember Baldwin.

It might be expected that I should attempt here a temperature chart of Neville Chamberlain's low spirits, but my occasional reference in this narrative to our official relations will have shown that I could hardly be an impartial judge. On the other hand, readers between the lines will have discerned that, in writing of "Mr. Gardiner's" descendants in my first chapter, I have had Chamberlain's personal virtues in mind, as well as his limitations. I think, indeed, that his record as Prime Minister will deserve a sympathetic reassessment by future historians more even, perhaps, than Baldwin's, if only because the reassessment of Baldwin's is already much farther advanced.

And what of the other major figure in the English public life of my time, Lloyd George, against whose exuberances our low spirits were an almost conscious reaction? I hardly know; perhaps Andrew Fairservice's epitaph is the best: "Ower bad for blessing and ower gude for banning, like Rob Roy."

2

The reader who has followed me thus far will no doubt reflect that the "great" men in politics whom I have known best have been the relatively unsuccessful – at least they have been men whose success did not stand the test of time. I suppose that is true, and I do not think I even regret it, low-spirited as my judgment may appear; for, in the setting of my times, success may well seem a word of little meaning. What meaning can it have when measured against the memory of the lost friends of one's youth? Of an earlier lost generation, Judge Holmes said seventy years ago: "In the portraits of those who fell in the civil wars of England, Vandyke has fixed on canvas the type of those who stand before my memory. Young and gracious figures, somewhat proud and remote, but with a melancholy and sweet kindness. There is upon their faces the shadow of approaching fate and the glory of generous acceptance of it." The language may be a little over-sentimental for a modern English taste; but it expresses memories which I remember being overwhelmingly revived for Judge Holmes thirty years later by a letter of Julian Grenfell's to his mother, which she sent on to him. "Generous acceptance" may, indeed, be the best virtue that such a generation has to bequeath to its survivors.

As a type of those survivors, I am tempted to say a word about a friend, whom I have already mentioned in my narrative, a man a little older than myself and much more high-spirited, very ambitious and sorely disappointed in his ambitions, who seemed to me to find in his last eight months of relative success a generosity and a gentleness – or, perhaps better, a *gentilesse* – which only a few intimates had recognized earlier to be the real foundations of his character. George Lloyd's biography has been written by one of those intimates and I am not entitled to add to it; but, if only because our political complexions seemed to differ so widely on the surface, I cannot be wholly silent about him.

Lloyd had the sort of ability – even the sort of genius – for which there is no room in English home politics; and that has always seemed to me to be the chief defect of the English parliamentary system. It gives no encouragement to natural administrative talent. Though Lloyd could lead others, he was essentially always a one-man team; he could not conciliate or put himself in committee. Nor could he take political issues with the customary grain of salt; he believed too passionately in the British Empire and in Tory social reform. He could not understand the apparently low temperatures of Baldwin's leadership. To his Indian ministers in Bombay and to his Foreign Office superiors while he was in Egypt he seemed arrogant, and there was enough of Mr. Darcy in him to make the judgment not wholly unjust. Yet what really offended them, unconsciously perhaps, was the touch of the prophet in him – and the Tory prophet is the most anomalous of political phenomena, the most difficult to fit into any system of Government. He was commonly derided, while he was in the East, for having a childish love of the 'red carpet"; but in truth he had something at once more valuable and more dangerous: a positive philosophy of the red carpet which he once expounded in India to a reluctant Prince of Wales. The ruler must endure his pedestal, especially in the East, in order that, on due occasion, he may step down from it for the greater encouragement of the ruled. To call that a philosophy of condescension is to mistake its whole character and motive, but it is a mistake that is only too easily made. Hence the red carpet joke.

Hence, too, Lloyd's curious discomfort in the mid-thirties in playing the part to which he was condemned in the controversy about Indian constitutional reforms, a discomfort which he concealed from the world but betrayed, I think, often to me. He was a dictatorial administrator in the tradition of John Lawrence, but he was also as convinced a constitutionalist as Halifax or Hoare. As Governor of Bombay, he had genuinely tried to work the Montagu-Chelmsford constitutional system, and his heart had been in the experiment. He thought any large extension of the experiment premature, mainly from his experience of the doubtful fitness of Indian ministers in the field of social policy, which was always his chief interest; but he could not share either Churchill's root-and-branch opposition to all constitutional innovations at the Centre, or his naive acceptance of the full Simon plan of Provincial Autonomy. The prophet in him made him a pungent controversialist on public platforms, but his speeches did not satisfy himself. He would much rather have taken a constructive part in framing the new constitution which he foresaw to be inevitable; and his chief disappointment in the whole business was that he did not receive the invitation to sit on the Joint Select Committee which he thought that Hoare had promised him.

He had felt the same discomfort during his years in Egypt. His administrative instinct could not adapt itself to the queer mixture of military occupation and diplomacy which was the Foreign Office's idea of regulating Anglo-Egyptian relations, nor, indeed, to the narrow traditions of the Cromer regime; yet his philosophy of the red carpet was here out of place, for he could have no responsibilities in Cairo which could justify a pedestal nor any administrative policy which could give him occasions to descend from it. Almost the only occasion of this kind that he could find was the introduction of good English teaching and influence into the new University of Cairo. In this he enlisted my help with English universities, not wholly unsuccessfully; but he always refrained from any attempt to enlist my politcal influence, partly no doubt because he rightly discounted it, but partly also because he was scrupulous about involving his friends in his personal dis-agreements with rhe Foreign Office about policy. Loyalty is a word of many meanings; Austen Chamberlain and the Foreign Office suspected Lloyd of political disloyalty, and so, I am afraid, did Baldwin, whose persistent cold-shouldering of him was, to me, his worst mistake in personal relations, even if it was not wholly unjustified; but in the best personal sense of the word, loyalty seemed to me to be his essential quality, and his discomfort was never greater than when, against his will, his dismissal from Cairo was made the occasion of a regrettable parliamentary debate. It was not until his last months as Secretary of State for the Colonies in time of war that his true qualities as an administrator in a constitutional government could be clearly seen; and in that office he will be long remembered by his colleagues and his subordinates, especially by the youngest of them.

I have written thus of Lloyd as a type of the survivors of a lost generation. That may seem to be a queer estimate of a man at once so individual and, be it confessed, so difficult; and, indeed, I doubt whether the more brilliant of my contemporaries, or near-contemporaries, who are most often mentioned as probable leaders had they survived, would ever have attempted political leadership as Lloyd did. Moreover, to use the phrase which has been appropriated recently by a younger politician, I do not think that most of them were "born to believe", as Lloyd certainly was. But I fancy that they would have shared all Lloyd's discomfort in making terms with the post-war world and might well have shared his failure. And I am sure that, if they had attempted the sort of success on which he had fixed his ambition, they would have accepted failure with the same generosity as he eventually did in his later years.

3

I pass to the memory of a very different man in another continent: Henry L. Stimson of New York. He was Baldwin's junior by one year and outlived him politically by eight; he entered public life as Federal District Attorney for New York two years before Baldwin entered Parliament, and he was a brilliantly successful war-time Secretary of War at Washington in his seventies, when Baldwin was in dishonoured retirement in Worcestershire; but, though the two men were so different both in character and career and, so far as I know, never met one another, they are always coupled in my memory as the two who, on the whole, best understood and felt the times in which they lived and, in their different ways, were the least unequal to them. Indeed, if they could have been rolled into one, the combination would have come near to my ideal of statesmanship for those times.

Stimson was no politician in the English parliamentary sense of the word. His only attempt at elected office was his unsuccessful campaign for the governorship of New York in 1910, which he himself has immortalized by recording Theodore Roosevelt's criticism of him at the time: "Darn it, Harry, a campaign speech is a poster, not an etching." He made a name for himself as an effective crusader on public platforms for political causes which transcended party issues, notably on the theme, so unpopular between the wars, of America's neglected responsibilities in international affairs; but the name won him respect, rather than popularity. Unlike Baldwin, he never sought to make or to manage a political party, or even to enjoy the fruits of his membership of one; and it says much for the essential virtues of the American political system that a man so independent and so unselfseeking should have held office under four administrations, twice as Secretary of War and once as Secretary of State, once as Governor General of the Philippines and once as head of a notably successful diplomatic mission in Central America. Such a combination of the professional lawyer and the independent political thinker on the outer fringes of active politics, ever available for a variety of public employments, can hardly be paralleled in modern English public life, where every man tends to have his own niche; the nearest analogies in our day would perhaps be a rare trade union leader or a figure like Sir Walter Monckton, and these analogies would be only superficial.

Stimson had much more natural "charm" than Baldwin and, in a way, he was much more English in his appetite for active recreation. In his early days he was known to his friends as a big game shot in the Rockies and later, while Baldwin would vegetate at Aix, he developed a taste for Scottish grouse moors. But he differed from Baldwin chiefly in the fact that he was, as he said of himself, a "man of executive mind". As an advocate of reforms, he was constantly intent on the strengthening of the executive branch of government and, as a man of action, on the mastery of administrative techniques and on the kind of judgment which makes those techniques effective. In this he possessed the most important quality which Baldwin undoubtedly lacked. But he shared intensely Baldwin's concern for the moral aspect of national and social policy and I think that, if anything, he surpassed Baldwin in combining this moral sense with a cool judgment which some politicians mistook for frigidity.

Looking back, I am surprised to realize how little I actually saw of Stimson through all these years. My knowledge of him at Washington in 1911–13, when he was first Secretary of War, was mainly indirect, especially through my most intimate Washington friend, now Justice Felix Frankfurter, a member of his staff and the pillar of the "House of Truth". Then I spent the Christmas week of 1917 with him in a small antiquated liner on the Atlantic, when I was coming home to consult with the Foreign Office and he was bound for the front as a Colonel of Artillery. I last saw him, I think, at a dinner party in London in 1930 when he was Secretary of State. There were twenty years between us, a difference of age which matters much when one is young. Yet, somehow, I always felt I knew him well, and my chief regret in life is that I missed the opportunity of dealing with him as ambassador when he was in charge of the foreign policy of the United States. But that is a trivial way of putting it. My real regret is for Stimson as a type of all the essential friendliness of America which so rarely found a way of expressing itself during these inter-war years and, whenever it made some advance in that direction, found so little response in Britain.

Genuine American disappointment with British policy, due largely, but not wholly, to misunderstanding, was, indeed, a real factor in the politics of those wasted inter-war years, of which Englishmen take too little account. At the risk of more senile wandering, I am tempted to adduce the memory of another great American in his old age, that of Justice Brandeis. I did not know him in his radical years before the first war, when he was campaigning against the "money power"; we made friends only after he came to Washington as a member of the Supreme Court. Great lawyer as he was, his political sense never seemed to me to be very strong, and his Zionism was always of a less realistic brand than Weizmann's. Indeed, he reminded me sometimes of the Victorian bishop's comment on a colleague, that he had heard often of the milk of human kindness, but had never before met the cow. But that is a disposition, common enough in the United States, with which English sophistication must learn to make terms if there is to be any future for Anglo-American relations. When I last saw him in 1930 he was pathetically pained by what he felt was the unsympathetic attitude of British officials in

Palestine towards the development of the "Jewish national home".
He had grown up in admiration of the spirit of British administrators overseas, and his belief in the "national home" had been in
large measure based on his confidence in that spirit. Now he
felt that our colonial civil service was degenerating. That was a
naïve misjudgment, but it did not entirely lack some justification.
It was only a little later that two other American Zionists, friends
of his, had to listen to Sidney Webb's indiscreet avowal (as one of
them reported it to me): "I have been in favour of the underdog
all my life, and I have come to the conclusion that the underdog in
Palestine is the Arab."

It was this gradual dissipation of the accumulated fund of
American friendliness that I regretted most in these years, rather
than the more superficial negligences and ignorances of professional politicians. When I was last in Washington in the spring of
1930, the efforts of the anti-isolationists to secure American
adherence to the Court of International Justice seemed to me to be
rather pathetically out of place. The real trouble was that, even
when Anglo-American relations were correct, there was as little
warmth in them as there was any kind of "zest" in the Hoover
Administration; and it was against this misunderstanding coolness,
even more than against American fear of war, that Franklin
Roosevelt had to struggle during his first seven years as President
between 1933 and 1940.

4

In one respect, I suppose that I myself am specially vulnerable to
the charge of low spirits. In my early days at the Board of Education, an old friend of mine, reviewing a book of educational
essays, to which I had contributed a preface, remarked that there
were few signs in the book, and certainly none in my preface, of
the renaissance in education for which a war-shattered world was
looking. That was true. *Renaissance* was the highbrow's version
of the simpler popular appetite for educational opportunity which
I have tried to describe in Chapter VI; and, as myself something

of a highbrow by origin, I was expected to understand and speak that language. Instead, I have always, I think, shared C. S. Lewis's dislike of it; and it has, moreover, seemed to me to be a peculiarly bad medium for expressing educational policy. If the teacher has anything to offer to the young it is the accumulated knowledge and experience of earlier generations; he may break continuity with the recent past in order to revive still older forgotten truths; but, even so, his new learning is apt to have results the reverse of what he intends. Thus the classical revival in Western Europe at the end of the Middle Ages, which has earned itself the title of The Renaissance *par excellence*, introduced a new pedantry into the schools no less than a new learning, as well as new fashions in politics in which the disillusioned survivors of the first World War could take little pride. They could, moreover I thought, take little pride either, for the reasons I have indicated, in the new educational philosophies or the bowdlerized history of their own day. I could, therefore, conceive of no educational policy, at any rate none within the reach of politicians, which did not consist essentially in the strengthening of an existing tradition and its wider sharing among those who had been hitherto denied access to it.

I had no reason to be ashamed of such a policy. Indeed, it came nearer, perhaps, to satisfying the popular appetite than most schemes of highbrow hankerers after an educational renaissance. But if it was to carry conviction, it had to be administered with generosity, and it was, no doubt, just that impression of generosity that I failed to convey. The future conservative administrator of education may well learn from that failure. His only distinctive asset is generosity. His opponents may be "progressive"; they may even be extravagant; but they are seldom generous in the best sense of the word. In the name of equality, they are apt to squeeze education within a compass narrow enough to be easily distributed in equal shares. Their sufficient objection to varieties in education, which may not be suited to all tastes and abilities, is to ask how candidates for such different types of school are to be selected. *A la carte* meals are troublesome both to cook and to serve; better a uniform pill that all can swallow – and that all can be compelled to swallow.

All educational reformers would, of course, repudiate any such calculation; nevertheless, those who allow themselves to be dominated by the idea of equality seem to fall inevitable, even if unwilling, victims to this tendency. In the last forty years or so, it has resulted in cutting off the public services of education, as they have been built up by all the English-speaking peoples, from the whole main cultural tradition of Western Europe, by barring the teaching of any foreign language, ancient or modern, to any child below the age of eleven, or even twelve or thirteen. As I write, this age seems likely before very long to be raised to fifteen at least; up to some such age children are to enjoy an equal share of a language-less education in a "comprehensive" school, in order that they may be spared from undergoing any form of earlier selective examination.

One does not need to be an old-fashioned classic or a devotee of the "eleven-plus examination" to see the dangers of a policy of equality so interpreted. It can be used to discourage an early grounding in mathematics as easily as in languages. With the consequent decay of the whole grammar school system built up since the Act of 1902, it bids fair to leave the independent preparatory and "public" schools to serve as the only remaining cultural bridge between England and the continent, and they, of course, will not long be allowed to survive. Such a disastrous *reductio ad absurdum* of the principles of equality cannot be averted by debate or argument; it can be averted only by men of more conservative mind who will demonstrate the possibilities of an alternative policy of generosity which closes no doors of access to learning, but opens them all more widely, and if I failed in that demonstration my responsibility is, indeed, a heavy one.

5

If I add one further retrospective comment on the public England of my day, it is with great diffidence, because I know I am not a competent witness to the facts. Sir Arthur Bryant, writing of the early nineteenth century, has comforted his readers for the drab colours of Liverpool's government and for the prevalent caddishness of English society after Waterloo by reminding them that a nation so poor in statesmanship and social manners could still find hope in the possession of a whole galaxy of literary genius.[1] This was not true, alas, of Baldwin's England; he may have turned his own lamp low, but at least his light was steadier than any flicker that poets or novelists could throw on his path. There was literary genius enough, but it seemed to have no heart in it; it lived in the Waste Land, among the Hollow Men. And I protest, in retrospect, that we politicians and the people we tried blunderingly to serve, low spirited though we might be, were better men than that, and lived in a brighter climate.

It was not, of course, that we expected praise, still less enthusiasm. On the contrary (as I once remember saying on a public educational platform, to the delight of old Quiller-Couch), one would have given much to see the left-wing writers of the day turn to Milton and Cobbett, to learn from them what good cursing really meant. Scorn may not be the best gift of poets, or even of sociological pamphleteers, but it has vivifying qualities. Siegfried Sassoon could strike this authentic note, but his growl seemed to be dying away in the 'twenties. So was Chesterton's heartier scorn; his heroics, which had appealed to me so much before and during the war, seemed to be losing themselves in an indiscriminate disgust of all policies and a contempt for all politicians, in that crackling of dry thorns under a Fascist pot which was to delude the bonfire-boys of Europe.

I say I am not a good judge of all this, for I come of the old-fashioned school that believes, with Dr. Johnson, that the function of literature is to teach men to enjoy life or to endure it; and there was little in all the literature of the 'twenties to hearten the oppressed or to console the unhappy or the perplexed. I am even so old-fashioned as to ask for eloquence in my poetry. That is what I had found in the Chesterton of the *Ballad of the White Horse*; and it made me impatient to be told by a poet-minister of

[1] *The Age of Elegance.*

Eire at an Imperial Conference dinner, that Verlaine had put a
stop to all that. *Prends l'éloquence et tords-lui le cou* must, he told me,
be the poet's gospel for these days. True the later Yeats was, at that
moment, denying this gospel in Eire itself; but I confess I still
preferred the easier eloquence of his earlier manner.

Nature abhors a vacuum, and this vacuum in the generous use
of language had somehow to be filled. It may not be entirely
fanciful to see Baldwin, in his more elegiac moods, as (to embroider one of Lloyd George's phrases about him) an unwilling
and lonely bardic figure against this lack-lustre background. A
Prime Minister ought not to be tempted, by lack of competition,
to stray too far into the regions of morals and imagination; and
Baldwin yielded only too easily to the temptation. To a Cornish
mass-meeting he liked to talk of Wesley, rather than of statesmanship; and perhaps one of his deepest thoughts was that the England
of his day needed a Wesley more than any political leader. But he
did not aspire to climb those heights himself and, in these moods,
he could only draw his eloquence from the past, from his love of
an old rural England and from memories of Abbotsford and
Dryburgh, after the manner of that heart-breaking minor poetry
of home-sickness which some of the "lost generation" of the
war had left behind them. Even in that, he stood almost alone;
of all my generation of poets, only Victoria Sackville-West, for
instance, could rise to the simplicities of a pastoral in the grand
manner.

This shyness of the imagination seems to me to have lasted
down nearly to the Silver Jubilee of 1935. The period found its
appropriate close in the artless rejoicings of those days; and
Baldwin, truth to tell, had by then little left to say. A younger
school of inarticulate angry men and half-articulate poets were to
find, in 1936 and later, a new release for their frustrated enthusiasms in the Spanish war. Release but, I fear, hardly utterance. To
people like myself, at least, this particular enthusiasm must seem
absurdly misconceived; yet, after all, some were prepared to die
for it – and that is enough.

One voice alone seemed to me to outlast that brief fever,

leaving me with, at any rate, two lines within my comprehension:

> "For what is done, not to be undone again.
> May the judgment not be too heavy upon us."[1]

[1] T. S. Eliot, *Ash-Wednesday*.

CHAPTER XII

A University, 1937-52

I

This chapter can be no more than a short postscript. Is it significant, I wonder, that I should feel so much more diffidence in writing of the university administration in which I passed the last fifteen years of my working life than of my political experiences in Cabinets and in the House of Commons? If, as I imagine, these were the years when I settled down to the sort of job for which I was best fitted and in which I did my most effective work, why do I not find more pleasure in expatiating upon them than upon my less successful wanderings in the political wilderness? Probably the reason is that a University has a continuing life of its own, a corporate personality more real than the shifting scenes of a party or a Cabinet or even, in these days, of the Mother of Parliaments. In such larger and more public scenes one may play one's part, without much feeling that one's work lives after one in the enduring life of the whole. Some, I know, do feel like that about the House of Commons, though I fancy that the feeling is rarer today than among an earlier generation, and I, at any rate, could never feel it. We all, no doubt, feel something like that, though more remotely, about the still larger units to which we owe our ulitmate loyalty: the nation and empire. But we have learnt the danger of Fichte's exhortation to Germans to find their "immortality" in their nation. Ordinary people at any rate, need a smaller and more tangible working home to which they can give their life and their affection; and only those nations are free or can "possess their soul in peace" which dare to honour and foster such lesser units of loyalty within themselves. But, just because one is more intimately committed to such working homes, one may well be as reluctant to write about them as about one's living friends or one's own family. If more men discovered this way of possessing their soul in peace, there might be less history to be written, and certainly there would be fewer autobiographies.

The working home where I settled down was the University of Durham, of which I was Vice-Chancellor for two years out of every four, and more especially its Newcastle Division (King's College) where I was directly responsible, as permanent Rector, for the education and welfare of some two-thirds of its members, including its only Medical School and its only departments of Applied Science. It was my first duty, in partnership with my colleague, the Warden of the Durham Division, to reorganize this dual university in accordance with Statutes newly drawn up by a Royal Commission; my second to take my part in expanding it in order to meet growing and changing demands. In the end, some time before my retirement in 1952, the dual university, with numbers more than doubled, had become, in effect, two combined universities, each of full university stature, responsible for its own teaching, discipline and welfare, its own staffing and its own building plans, each (in practice) administering its own Treasury grants, and combined with the other only for the purpose of conferring degrees, with all the faculty regulations and examinations incident thereto.

My colleague and I differed about the constitutional changes appropriate to the new facts and, as I write four years after my retirement, the Combined Universities are still hesitating to emerge. Having failed to solve that constitutional problem before retirement, it would be irresponsible for me to discuss it now that I can be no more than an "indolent reviewer". It is not, perhaps, very important. I mention it only because the dilemma betrayed, no doubt, my own aptitudes and my own weaknesses. I began by a genuine effort to focus the reorganized university, in the spirit of its revised statutes, as a new and powerful academic body, combining the civic and provincial virtues, in the one unit, of a Redbrick University, with the collegiate tradition and pattern, in the other, of a miniature Oxford or Cambridge. But, at the end of the

war, I found myself increasingly absorbed in the administrative
task of developing Redbrick, and increasingly doubtful whether
its association with the other unit could ever be more than
diplomatic. I do not think that this was entirely due to Mr. Darcy's
inveterate preference for being king at Pemberley rather than a
partner in any larger enterprise. I would sooner say that the lesser
loyalties of a free nation lose their savour if they are not kept
within the bounds of reality and intimacy; as soon as they succumb
to the temptations of empire-building, even on a modest scale,
they begin to claim a privileged place in the community, instead
of being content to feed the hidden springs that water its roots.
The whole history of the trade union movement seems to point
that moral. Or, if this language be thought to exaggerate the
worst that the State in this country has to fear from university
empire-building, let us simply say that academic polygamy does
not work; that a wife is a whole-time job, and so is one of Matthew
Arnold's ideal academies; and that the chief administrator of such
an academy had usually better take as his motto Chesterton's "I
am not wise enough to rule so small a thing".

I am afraid I felt this even more about the national Committee
of Vice-Chancellors and Principals than about the Senate and the
Faculty Boards of what seemed to me to be the somewhat
imaginary University of Durham. As a politician, I had often
lamented the absence of any national body which could think out
and represent university policy; and my first experience of the
then nascent Vice-Chancellors' Committee had been as a political
visitor when, in the 'twenties, on behalf of George Lloyd, I had
tried to interest it in the University of Cairo, and when, later in the
'thirties, I had recourse to it in planning the academic side of the
British Council's work. In the 'forties, when I saw it from the
inside, the pressures of war and demobilization made such a
Committee on University policy indispensable and I think it did
excellent work in placing the universities at the disposal of the
Government in the ways, and within the limits, where they could
be of the greatest service. At the end of the war, too, it initiated
(if inspired begging deserves that name) the novel idea of capital

grants from the Treasury, without which the universities could not have faced the task of expansion to meet the needs of demobilization. But, useful as it was and is, I never felt that it represented the peculiar qualities in each university which could alone justify what was fast becoming a new privileged class in an egalitarian democracy. Indeed, its greatest virtue was that it did not try to do so. It was content to be a mere business committee and to hold itself in reserve for emergencies. Yet, even so, a university policy is not a university community and those who are too intent on devising the first may not have the time to create the second.

I claim no more for these views than that they betray my own limitations. Of course, my "hen-with-one-chick" attitude has its dangers. A professorial friend once laughed, not unkindly, at my administration of King's College as a record of "enlightened buccaneering", and that may be true. Moreover, most academic husbands are relatively short-lived; their wives can fairly expect to get a full-time one occasionally, but not a new one every ten or fifteen years; they had better learn to stand on their own feet. Yet, all the same, a university which, deprived of an active head, learns the habit of subjection to its own faculties may find itself in even worse case – and such lapses are not unknown.

2

The chief purpose of my buccaneering in the last seven years or so of my tenure as Rector of King's College was to meet the post-war demand for an expanded production of scientists and technologists. I could never see much sense in the idea of founding one or more "technological universities"; those who advocated such projects had commonly little experience of English Red-bricks and did not realize to what extent they were already the English version of American Institutes of Technology and the *Technische Hochschulen* of Central Europe. But if there was any Redbrick university which seemed called at the end of the war to become a model institute of science and technology, it was surely King's College. As Armstrong College, before the reorganization, it had already won a distinguished reputation in engineering,

o

in mining, and in naval architecture; as the new King's College, it had come to embrace also, in its Medical School, the most liberal of the sciences and the most humane of the technologies. From its modest, and sometimes disturbed, beginnings, it seemed, moreover, to have derived a keener instinct for both diversification and integration than most other universities; and it had shown in the war a peculiar capacity for self-mobilization in face of unexpected tasks. Its own Faculty of Arts was strong enough to leaven the technological lump, the more so because it had shown a tendency to develop especially the applied arts in architecture, archaeology and fine art; and its association with Durham gave it an exceptional opportunity to strike a balance between literary and scientific studies.

From these beginnings, my buccaneering in technological waters was not unsuccessful; but the chief lesson it taught me was that a university of the English type, new or old, starting with even the greatest initial advantages, can make only a limited contribution to the development of technological studies. As chairman of a Ministry of Education Committee in the last year of the war, I had already guessed at this conclusion and my later experience confirmed it. For one thing, the "honours" system in English universities is a handicap (I say "English" deliberately, for the Scottish university tradition is rather different), especially as it had come to be reinforced between the wars by a system of individual post-graduate research based upon the introduction of the Ph.D. "higher" degree. It threw all the emphasis of university education on the attainment of a high standard of individual excellence in particular fields of study, and, as the standard tended continually to rise, the chosen fields of study tended, as continually, to narrow. This honours standard tended, too, to be reflected in the teaching of every subject even at a lower than honours level, as a subsidiary subject in other degree courses. This became most evident, perhaps, in the teaching of the pure sciences to candidates for degrees in applied science and medicine, even though the main courses for these degrees at Newcastle were not themselves honours courses. The staffing of a department of mathematics, for example, would be determined by the requirements of an Honours School of Mathematics; and the standard of mathematical teaching to engineers would be insensibly and almost unconsciously strained in consequence. In a somewhat different spirit, an Honours School of English would disclaim any competence to teach engineering students how to write clear English prose.

These tendencies could be corrected. I think they were, in fact, largely corrected in my time, though not through any action of mine, in the teaching of pure science to medical students. But the broad truth remained, that a university is not, and to a large extent cannot be, staffed or organized to produce *educated men and women in quantity*. It is inevitably too much concerned to produce *scholars in quality*. All teaching and all examinations must inevitably be conducted in a constant tension between, on the one hand, the old adage that the purpose of education is to teach the student to think for himself and, on the other hand, the exasperated injunction of my Eton tutor to his pupils that they must not presume to *think* until they had become scholars. University teaching and examination are often too much biassed in the first direction, being directed, even in a student's freshman year, to encourage premature thought rather than to elicit verified knowledge.

It is natural that, in days when men are more and more inclined to worship equality, universities should cling, though sometimes indiscriminately, to this honours standard of individual excellence. But it may also be salutary that a makeshift academician like myself should question the validity of an excellence so judged. Certainly, among my contemporaries from about the beginning of the century, excellence so academically judged hardly seems to me to have corresponded very closely with any practical standard of competence in employments traditionally recruited from the older universities, like the Indian Civil Service. Excellence in a university is, after all, derived, not directly from the form of its degree courses, but from its sense of the central purpose which those courses are intended to serve. In the Oxford of my day, no undergraduate could escape the feeling that a university existed to train a governing class in Church and State. Whatever might be our chosen subjects of study, our thoughts were naturally of *government*, our drive was towards problems of public policy; and, in a university dominated by such honours courses as "Greats" and History, we ran, perhaps, little risk of supposing that government and policy could be matters of any narrow specialization. If, as I think, this central purpose, which had been sufficient to lend assurance and balance to an old academic governing class, was beginning, in my day, to be blurred by the turbulent questionings of a new sociology, it had not quite lost its influence. If Oxford had had any definable reason for existence, it still obviously existed to train men of executive mind. But, in the newer Redbricks, no corresponding sense of purpose had yet enlivened the drudgeries of technology, a study certainly requiring executive qualities no less than older studies in political thought. Pure science, indeed, had been developing its own ideology, the ideology of the lonely explorer and pioneer; but its best representatives were too often of the type of Lord Rutherford, who would pursue the atom with all the perseverence, and sometimes the exuberance, of an old fox-hunting squire, but who abominated any attempt to relate his favourite sport to anything so pretentious as a philosophy. This was obviously not good enough for the technologist who must find his central purpose in the application of science to the advancement of a mechanical civilization and to the evolution of a corresponding way of life for thousands of his fellow-citizens in factory, mine and farm, if not in society as a whole. In this sense, no technologist worth his salt can forgo philosophy or can escape being a humanist. Humanists of an older school may deride his love of machines, but American universities are beginning to show the world that a passion for machines may be a better way of approach to a new humanism than, for instance, the logic-chopping of some recent fashions in honours schools of philosophy.

I did not doubt – especially as I saw the situation at Newcastle developing – that English universities would eventually find their way to give to technological studies the same kind of impulse and the same kind of inspiration; but I did doubt whether they could find it alone and whether they could convey the impulse and the inspiration to all who would need it in the industrial civilization of tomorrow. That is why I always regretted the premature dissolution, over the past half-century, of so many independent, or nearly independent, non-university centres of technological teaching, such as Coopers Hill and some London colleges, who sheltered under the capacious umbrella of the City and Guilds, while offering free scope to good teachers; as well as the concentration of all such teaching either in universities or in technical colleges administered by local education authorities. Municipal administration, even at its best, is not suited to higher education; its bias towards the child and the school is too strong. And in post-war days when inexperienced Labour education committees were putting their own too literal interpretation on the dangerous principle of "all power to the ratepayers", this municipal administration was becoming a positive threat to the free development of higher standards in technological teaching. Busy as I was with such development in a university, my chief regret was that the Government showed so little appreciation of the main recommendation of my Committee: for the supplementation of universities by a select body of self-governing Colleges of Higher Technology, undistracted either by university inhibitions or by municipal empire-building.

That regret deepened as I came to see more and more of university inhibitions after the war. One of these was the unanimous insistence of the Vice-Chancellors' Committee that no institute of technology should aspire to any kind of "parity" with universities unless it could develop faculties of Arts and Science as well as of Applied Science. Here the mistake lay, I think, in the use of the word "faculty", with all its "honours" implications. There is much to be said for a steady resistance to monotechnics, claiming equality with universities. But a full technological education is itself far broader, or ought to be, than any faculty specializations and might, if properly developed, deserve better the title of higher education than a mere multiplicity of Honours Schools. Again,

one of the essential aims of Redbrick universities had been to
liberalize, and infuse scientific knowledge into, local provincial
life; yet at the end of the war King's College was, I think, the
only university that deplored the severance, then brought about
by the Government, between the teaching of agricultural science
and the provincial agricultural advisory service. Also, it was the
only university Medical School that was prepared to assume direct
responsibility for its teaching hospital in the new National Health
Service. That might, or might not, have been a good solution of
an, as yet, hardly solved problem; but, both in agriculture and in
medicine the reluctance of universities to undertake public responsibilities marked, I felt, a dangerous tendency to retreat into
academic seclusion.

3

These general considerations of policy were, however, only at
the back of my mind and, after my Government Committee had
published its recommendations, I took little part in pressing them
upon the attention of my university colleagues or the public. I had
had my fill of policies in earlier life; my business now was to
translate them into terms of the administration of one small university community. Policies may soon become unrecognizable
when thus translated; but the life of such a community is what
matters, for it is the end-product of all policies and outlasts them
for good or ill. Nay, in a sense, it confirms or discredits them.
That is the feeling that still inclines me to end my life as a Conservative, as, in the scene referred to in my first chapter, it inclines
me to side with my father rather than with Beatrice Webb, though
in terms of national policies I might agree more often with her than
with him. Almost the most tragic among my friends in these latter
days was, I think, Harold Laski whose heart was in his teaching at
the London School of Economics, where he is remembered with
affection by so many of his students, but who could not resist the
temptation of foraying into national politics, where his genius for
scholarship and for private friendship could only turn to petulance.
Earlier, in my Board of Education days, he had once shocked an

annual meeting of the National Union of Teachers by saying that
it was one of the purposes of education to teach indiscipline. This
is the old temptation of the intellectual to *épater le bourgeois*. "You
do not know what truth is," Bernard Shaw had once exploded in
the face of a Fabian colleague who had vamped up a loose piece of
economic writing; "truth is agony and bloody sweat". That story
was told me long afterwards, in 1914, by another Fabian pioneer,
Graham Wallas, who, in his academic retirement, was comment-
ing sadly on the extent to which Shaw had forgotten his own
precept. Wallas himself, who had impressed my youth enor-
mously by the wisdom and "strong benevolence of soul" of
an ex-revolutionary, startled me once later, at a large conference
at the Board of Education, by what I can only describe as an
epileptic frenzy of irrelevant secularist suspicion, called forth by a
perfectly innocent proposal. University life and thought may be a
powerful solvent of opinionated prejudices; I have seen that in a
provincial community and have caught a glimpse of it amid the
apartheids of South Africa, English and Dutch, and black and
white; but the solvent can only work slowly and those who possess
the secret of it are wise to resist the temptation to harden by
public advocacy or opposition the very prejudices which it is their
academic mission to dissolve.

This may sound like an over-quietist ideal; but, since it is mine,
I was fortunate in heading a university community at Newcastle
which, before I came there, already seemed to come very close to
it. I hope I did little to disturb that integrity and something,
perhaps, to strengthen it – though not nearly as effectively as the
influx of ex-service students, who, in the five years or so after the
war, went far to transform its manners and its spirit. So far as its
teaching staff were concerned its virtues had been friendliness and
a sometimes exaggerated pastoral sense of the overmastering
responsibility for good teaching; its defects, perhaps, had been a
certain insensitiveness to the claims of research, not entirely
justified even by the extreme inadequacy of its buildings, and an
over-coyness in attempting any kind of social leadership. I think I
did something, though only indirectly, to remove that reproach,

and to bring King's College more into the centre of the life of Northumberland and Tyneside; but I could not respond very heartily to Harold Laski's congratulation to me on my accession, which took the form of a wistful question, reminiscent of Beatrice Webb: "surely a Tyneside university must have something better to do than to turn out second-rate engineers and doctors." I could not resist a retort after the manner of Abraham Lincoln, that the Almighty must after all, have a liking for second-rate people, since He had made so many of them. Probably we two did not differ much in practice; but I could never rid myself of the feeling that the excellence aimed at by a university must include an intelligent sympathy for the useful drudgeries which are the inevitable lot of nine-tenths of its students.

In mere organization, the process of building a centre of university teaching in technology, with medicine and applied art as its natural allies, could have no general interest; and I will not try to sketch it here. I suppose, in fact, that if my name is remembered at all in a future University of Newcastle, it will be associated mainly, by no choice of my own, with plain bricks and mortar. I built much after the war (though not nearly as much as I could have wished); and, with the help of an understanding City Council, I was able to use the Town Planning Acts in order so to expand the university site that its teaching buildings and its hospitals may, in the fullness of time, come to dominate the northern entrance to the city, instead of lurking unnoticed on their hidden hilltop, behind a screen of mean shops and miscellaneous business premises. I say, by no choice of my own, for, essential as my building and planning were, as was also my multiplication of specialist professorships, I hope I always regarded them as no more than so many opportunities for giving scope to *personality*. The buildings were to give scope, not only to those who would dilate in them, so to speak, hereafter, but, in the immediate present, to a vigorous school of architecture, and especially to its very able professor, for they were nearly all home-produced, if one may use that phrase. And as to the professorships the obvious example of what I intended was the first new one that I engineered, thanks to the generosity of the Nuffield Provincial Hospitals Trust; the first full-time Chair of Child Health in the country, which was successful in giving a more than national scope to my friend and counsellor, Sir James Spence, to whom I, and the whole university, owe a moral, as well as an intellectual, debt which I cannot begin to express here.

If his is the only name that I can bring myself to mention here, it is because my other debts are so largely due to living friends who are still deep in the work which I have left. I am not, indeed, entitled to speak at all of that work in the first person singular; throughout, it was the work of a team of senior and junior colleagues, who should justly have the credit for the creation of, I hope, a new university. If I have anything personal to record here, let it be my farewell address to my last batch of graduating students at Newcastle in June 1952:

"A Graduation Address is necessarily a farewell, a farewell to those who are setting out on their life's work. Mine today is a farewell in a double sense; forgive me, then, if I speak rather personally.

"For some years past, you have been preparing yourselves to exercise power over others. That is the distinctive purpose of university education. For some of you, it may be the direct power of command; for others the subtler power of expert knowledge. Most of you will always occupy a quite humble place in the community; but it will usually be a place where you will, in some degree, be responsible for the management of other people's lives.

"Such power is dangerous. When Lord Acton said that 'all power corrupts' he was thinking of the power of command; but the warning is equally true of the power of knowledge. It is a danger to all who use it and to all on whom it is used. The modern world is staggering under the burden, not only of misused authority in government, but, even more, of misused knowledge. You have graduated today into that danger; you leave behind you a university still intent on leading your successors, in their turn, into the same danger.

"This danger, neither you nor your university can escape. We cannot escape it by running away from it. The use of power is our allotted talent; we dare not bury it in a napkin. Nor can we escape it by shutting our eyes to it, by professing smugly, as is the fashion today, that our use of power is merely 'service'. Let us beware of abstractions. That has been the favourite language of tyrants. There have been no worse enemies of freedom, in action or in thought, than powerful men who have called themselves 'public servants' or 'servants of truth'. Service, in any real sense, means obedience; it means doing personally for a master, not what you think is good for him, but what he requires of you. We cannot honestly acknowledge our fellow-men to be our masters in this personal sense; it is the bad teacher who teaches only what his pupils want to learn; the bad doctor who tells his patients only what they want to hear; the bad politician who waits for public opinion to tell him what to do. Still less can we take as our master some personal dictator, or even what Englishmen characteristically call 'a Service', where every man is a link in a chain of command. We cannot all be civil servants and, even if we could, bureaucracy may be as great a danger to freedom as dictatorship. Yet it remains true that the only man who can be safely trusted with command over free men, in action or in thought, is the free man who knows himself to be in personal obedience to a master.

"This is the dilemma of what Englishmen call democracy. It has been the tradition of English universities to bring men up to live consciously in this dilemma without being afraid of it – to strike, for themselves, the right balance between authority and freedom, to use power without presumption, but without diffidence. On the whole we of the English universities have not done this too badly; but for some years past we have been doing it too much by instinct and too little by reason. We are better, no doubt, than we used to be at giving our students a knowledge of social and scientific facts, but much worse than we used to be at giving them any idea how to set those facts in order.

We are urged today to 'educate for management', but that too often means the management of accounts and machines; to each succeeding university generation, the *respectful management of men* is becoming more and more a habit or a knack, and less and less a philosophy. But habit is not enough, especially now when our old liberal democracy is being challenged by a new kind of democracy with an all too definite philosophy of totalitarian power.

"That philosophy does not bother men with balances and dilemmas; on the contrary, in the words of Rousseau, it declares war on 'all institutions which set a man in conflict with himself'; in the Marxist language of 'dialectical materialism', it delivers men from the burden of conscience by teaching them that the 'interpenetration of opposites' is merely the necessary condition of all human thought. Against this, our instinct is still that the good governor or the good citizen must never lose his sense of the real and fundamental conflict between his best ideals and his exercise of power over his fellow-men. 'As I would not be a slave', wrote Abraham Lincoln at the very height of his almost dictatorial power, 'so I would not be a master. Whatever differs from this, to the extent of the difference, is no democracy.' But if this is only a habit of mind, it may easily become a habit of hypocrisy. Ever more and more urgently we need a language in which to express it as a rational belief.

"There is only one such language. The philosophy of a balance between authority and freedom is, not only in history but in reason, a Christian philosophy. That is, not only its native, but its natural, language. The most remarkable spectacle, I think, in all modern history is the way in which Lincoln, himself no orthodox believer, was driven to use this language to express his political principles. But here again, let us beware of abstractions. The essence of this language is its shattering personal force. It is the language of personal obedience to a personal Master; of human nature in process of being remade through personal union with Him; of a brotherhood, thus united and thus changing, where freedom is claimed as His personal gift and authority exercised by His personal commission. Plainly, this language can never be an official one anywhere but in the Church of Christ itself. It cannot be the official language of the State; de-personalized into political terms, it, too, has often been the language of tyrants who, like Dostoievski's Grand Inquisitor, have governed in the name of Christ, but not in His obedience. But, if it cannot be the official language of the State, it must, in a liberal democracy, be at least a familiar language among statesmen. So, too, it cannot be the official language of any university, tempting as it is to use it so. How better, at first sight, could one express one's ideal of the aim and character of a good university than in the words of St. Paul: 'That we may be no longer children, carried about by every wind of doctrine, but, speaking the truth in love, may grow up together in all things.' But we dare not officially carry on this quotation to its personal conclusion, without which the rest may be but a vain aspiration: 'may grow up in all things into Christ, Who is the Head'. Yet, for myself, I have believed, and have come more and more to believe, that no modern university can be trusted with its immense privileges and responsibilities where this full language of Christian faith is not freely spoken by all who care to learn it. If I have ever had a university policy beyond bricks and books and engines and microscopes, it has been to foster a community in which such learning shall be easy. And to that learning I make bold to commit you now, with any power of blessing permitted to an expiring Vice-Chancellor – and, through that learning, to the sense, so rare in our stumbling Western world today, that, having this personal obedience, we have also a hope for mankind beyond the reach of all mere planners of power, and that, in this hope, amid the shaking of all things, we have in truth 'received a kingdom that cannot be moved'."

Index